PROCRASTINATION NATION

Gloria Arenson, MS, MFT, DCEP

Published by:
BrockArt Books
Santa Barbara, California

Procrastination Nation

Published by:
BrockArt Books, Santa Barbara, California
Printed in the United States of America. All rights reserved.

Caveat / Disclaimer

The information, instructions or advice presented are not intended to be a substitute for professional medical or psychological care. If you are under medical or psychological supervision, consult your health care professional before using any of the procedures in this book.

The author and publisher disclaim any liability or loss incurred directly or indirectly as a result of the use or application of any of the contents of this book.

Library of Congress Cataloging-in-Publication Data
Arenson, Gloria
Procrastination Nation / Gloria Arenson.
164 p. 13.97 x 21.59 cm. Includes bibliographical, resource references.
ISBN:978-0-9621942-5-2
1. Compulsive behavior.
Library of Congress Control Number: 2008904070

Cover and book design by Laurence T. Brockway, MA

Praise for Procrastination Nation

"If you need this book, you will probably never get around to reading it. But if you do, and if you follow its guidance, you will no longer need it (though you will be left with an invaluable tool you will also be able to apply in many other areas of your life).
David Feinstein, PhD, Author, *Energy Psychology Interactive* and *The Promise of Energy Psychology*

"Gloria Arenson is a pioneer in Energy Psychology, and her insights are eagerly sought by leaders in the field. In this book, she applies these breakthrough methods to procrastination, which is one of the biggest blocks to happiness, health and abundance. The methods in Procrastination Nation can quickly shift even the most stubborn self-defeating patterns, and shift the guilt that underlies this compulsion. You will be amazed at how, using these methods, even life-long procrastination can be eliminated. So leave the Procrastination Nation and liberate your genius with Gloria's powerful advice!"
**Dawson Church, PhD, Author,
*The Genie in Your Genes***

"Once again, Gloria Arenson takes the pressing and disabling problem of procrastination and not only explains why we do it, but provides simple and effective solutions to overcome it. Don't procrastinate-- get this book now and start using it: you'll be happy you did!"
Hyla Cass M.D. author, *8 Weeks to Vibrant Health* (www.drcass.com)

"While everyone procrastinates at times, chronic procrastination can be the bane of your life. In Procrastination Nation, Gloria Arenson reveals the multi-faceted causes of procrastination and offers a highly effective integration of EFT and cognitive therapy solutions. This book could very well save you a lot of time and misery."
Fred P. Gallo, PhD, Author of *Energy Tapping for Trauma* and founder of *Advanced Energy Psychology*

Procrastination Nation

FRED P. GALLO, PHD

Books By Gloria Arenson

How to Stop Playing the Weighting Game

A Substance Called Food: How to Understand, Control and Recover From Addictive Eating

Born To Spend

Five Simple Steps to Emotional Healing

Freedom At Your Fingertips

Procrastination Nation

Dedication

To my husband, Laurence Brockway, with love and appreciation for your support and collaboration. You are truly the inspiration for this book.

Acknowledgements

This book could not have been written without the cooperation of the wonderful people who have attended my classes and workshops for over twenty-five years and have freely shared their stories. I am grateful to my clients, people who are courageous in their determination to free themselves from procrastination. I hope their stories will inspire you.

I thank my wonderful husband whose generosity allowed me to study "up close and personal," the trials and tribulations of a longtime procrastinator/perfectionist. His willingness to allow me to share anecdotes about him makes him even more special to me.

I offer respect and admiration to Gary Craig for creating EFT, a technique that has changed my life and allowed me to help so many others. Thank you also to Cynthia Anderson for her outstanding coaching,

The case histories included in this book are based on the lives of real people. I have disguised some facts to protect their confidentiality. Sometimes I have combined or simplified cases to present a point more clearly. Procrastinators are members of both sexes. To remain nonsexist in my writing I have used male and female pronouns interchangeably when speaking of people in a general sense.

Procrastination Nation

Contents

Chapter 1

I Had to Write This Book

I would not be writing this book if it had not been for a colossal act of procrastination in my life. I started out in life as someone who accomplished what I said I would do and finished things on time. I was not a procrastinator. You could count on me to get the job done. I could count on myself.

In childhood, I developed a tendency toward perfectionistic expectations of myself at school. I don't know where it came from, certainly not from my parents, who didn't pressure me to adhere to an impossible standard. Yet I was drawn to the ideal of all A's as a moth is to a flame and filled myself with worries of not living up to my own expectations of myself. I thrived on competition in high school and college the way an athlete enjoys the challenges of an exciting game against well-matched opponents. My motto was, "Difficult things should be easy for me." Surprisingly, my need to shine academically led me to a life changing experience.

I had fallen in love with the past when I was seven years old and continued to study ancient art and archeology in college. When graduate school beckoned, I was accepted at Columbia University in New York City, my hometown. I felt as if I was finally on the A team, getting ready for the big time. Archeology is a pretty small field where everyone knows everyone else in that specialized world, and archeology classes or seminars at Columbia at that time had an average of 6 or 7 students enrolled. There was nowhere to hide if you weren't prepared, but I was an optimistic competitor.

One spring semester I signed up for an intriguing seminar titled "Art of the Russian Steppes." I looked forward to the adventure of learning. The first day, I timidly walked into the classroom and saw an enormous table that took up almost the entire room. That wasn't what astounded me most. What stunned me was the sight of the professor reclining odalisque-like on the table. He lay on his side with his cherubic bearded face supported by his bent arm.

"Oh, my God, what am I in for," I thought. Prim and proper student that I was then, I was intimidated at having an exalted scholar act in such a whimsical way. I got my second surprise of the day when I saw that the large green chalkboards that extended along two long walls were covered with either Chinese or Russian notations.

The professor saw the look of dismay on our faces and told us that since the Russian Steppes is an area shared by China and Russia, Russian or Chinese archeologists had done all the excavations. Inside my head, I heard my inner voice screaming, "How can I get an A? I've got to get an A!" I panicked. How could I do the reading if nothing was in English? Did I know someone who read Russian or Chinese who could translate for me? No!

I can't remember much about the next few weeks except that I was terribly worried and had nightmares and trouble sleeping. I turned into a super procrastinator because I simply couldn't figure out a way to get through this course, let alone get an A. I began putting off doing any work. I cut classes. I became increasingly morose. My fear grew. I froze. Since I was supposed to be able to overcome any and all challenges, I was too embarrassed to even talk to the professor and tell him my worries. Finally, I decided to drop the course. I had never dropped a course in my life.

My fear of failure and humiliation escalated to the point that I took a leave of absence from graduate school. I ran away, far away. That Summer I visited relatives in California and never returned home. Not only that, I didn't go back to New York City at all for the next 20 years. I did not complete the course, graduate or ever return to studying archeology! I procrastinated myself into a new life, entirely different from what I had imagined only months before. I married, had a family, became a psychotherapist and learned how to deal with living people rather than dead ones.

About 30 years later, I was teaching a class about procrastination and perfection. One evening I had an epiphany. As I was telling this story of my own procrastination, I suddenly realized that the other six students who stayed in the seminar had most likely passed the course. There was a way to succeed, and I could have discovered it if I stayed. For the first time in all those years I understood that most people's lives are not based on the belief that difficult things should be easy and that if you don't get an A you're a failure, even though I was able to point out this error in thinking to others.

Maybe I didn't become an archeologist, however my interest in exploring the origins of human culture still comes in handy in my psychotherapy practice. My favorite professor in college eloquently described how archeologists excavate the treasures that have been buried for thousands of years from beneath the ground and use special brushes to gently wipe away the mud and dirt that have covered them all this time. Finally, the golden object is revealed, as bright and shining as the day it was buried. That is how I see my clients. They were born perfect and golden. However, life has thrown dirt on them. Some have had their wonderful essence blighted at an early age and don't even know that underneath the dirt of misery, abuse and low self esteem lies the special person they once were. Psychotherapy is the brush I now use.

Over the years I have explored our present civilization and tried to comprehend what makes us do what we do even if it leads to a life of tragedy and self-sabotage. Instead of studying artifacts, I study thoughts and feelings. There must be a reason, an event, or belief to explain the destructive behaviors like procrastination that cause so much pain. My efforts led me to write books explaining the dynamics of and treatment for compulsive eating, purging, spending, and now procrastination.

When I teach classes about overcoming procrastination I write this sentence on the board: *Procrastination is your way of avoiding your fantasy of reality.* What I hope my students will realize at the end of the class is that negative behaviors tell us something symbolically about what isn't going well in our lives. Procrastination is all about avoidance. We must ask ourselves what we are avoiding and why. More than this, our actions are actually reactions to our personal view of the world as we perceive it, usually a negative one filled with critical people and dangerous situations, and our disapproving perception of ourselves. We have never checked our decisions out with others and thus hold these thoughts as truths. The result is a life of emotional pain and low self-esteem.

Sometimes I ask myself if my life-changing crisis was a curse or a blessing. At the time, it seemed to be a catastrophe since it ended what I thought was going to be my career. About twenty years later, I happened to see a television documentary detailing the life of a woman archeologist who was my age. At first I felt jealous and thought, "That should have been me!" As I watched, I was filled with gratitude that my life had taken another path. I was not meant for outdoor adventures in the blazing sun or for the life of an academic.

Some might say that God or the Universe closed that door. However, if you look carefully, you will notice that I closed it! I told myself that it was all or nothing, and once I left school I could never return. That was not the case. The university would have let me continue when I was ready to go back. It was not my pride but my fear that wouldn't let me.

As you read this book I hope that you will observe the ways you put things off without judging yourself, but with a wish to understand your actions with compassion. You will gain the ability to recognize why you act that way and discard what no longer benefits you. Procrastination can be a blessing in disguise. The choice is yours.

Chapter 2

Procrastination: The Waiting Game

We all seem busier than ever these days, living life in a fast lane. We have turned into a nation of multi-taskers. We have also turned into a procrastination nation since, for many of us, there isn't enough time to catch up. A little procrastination won't ruin your life, but sometimes it becomes a problem and keeps you from having the life you were meant to have. This book will show you an easy way to come to terms with the stresses of procrastination and overcome this common problem.

Putting things off or not finishing are behaviors that many of us adopt to avoid uncomfortable feelings of pain, guilt, shame, anxiety or fear. Procrastinators come in all sizes and shapes, young and old, all colors, denominations, from all walks of life and many cultures. Procrastinators are not stupid, weak, or bad.

Procrastination is not a disease although procrastinators rarely seem to be able to recover from it. If you Google the word procrastination, you will discover that we tend to view procrastination as a horrendous condition, impossible to conquer. It is so daunting that, according to experts on many different websites, we should seek to: avoid it, trick it, manage it, get around it, learn to live with it, structure it, control it, reduce it or push past it. As a psychotherapist with over twenty-five years experience, I know that it is possible to put an end to this behavior.

It's a Compulsion

Telling a procrastinator to buy a Blackberry or Day Planner to keep track of her life is like telling someone with depression to just think happy thoughts. It is more than a bad habit. It's not about using Willpower. Procrastination is a compulsion. One of my specialties is treating people who suffer from compulsive behaviors, especially compulsive overeating, binge purging, spending, debting, smoking, and Internet addiction to chat rooms and porn sites.

My definition of compulsion is: **If you cannot control when you start or when you stop a substance or behavior, you have a compulsion.** Technically, we might say that compulsion is self-induced changes in neurotransmission that result in problem behaviors. That means that our behavior affects our brain, which then affects our behavior. Then it turns into what looks like a bad habit.

I view procrastination as a compulsion because it is a behavior that people cannot control. It is a compulsion to not do. Putting things off is also a solution to other problems. Once I understood that dynamic, I decided to apply the same approach with procrastinators that I use with other compulsive clients. The unstoppable urge to overeat compulsively, spend compulsively, or engage in other activities without being able to control it is usually triggered by a kind of stress that results from feeling powerless and angry because of a situation or relationship that you can't change. I call this Super Stress.

All compulsive people, including procrastinators, are looking for a way out of the discomfort of Super Stress. Addicts use pleasure to medicate their pain while procrastinators use avoidance. Avoidance takes many forms. As a procrastinator, you may also turn to overeating, spending, drinking, etc as a distraction that keeps you away from the project that you should be working on. It is also easy to get lost in a book, hobby, TV show, the internet, DVDs, CDs, podcasts or phone calls rather than buckle down to the job you are putting off. Some of my clients have even escaped into sleep.

Who's In Charge?

After years of working with procrastinators, I realized that few put off undertakings in every area of their lives. Some people delay more at work, and others dawdle in their private lives. I maintain that there is no such thing as LAZY. Lazy is what *they* called you when you weren't doing what *they* wanted you to do ---pick up your clothes, put your toys away, write thank you notes, or practice the piano. I refer to this behavior as, *I don't wanna and you can't make me!* I will talk more about this in a later chapter.

That brings me to an important question, who are *they*? *They* are the people who were in charge of you when you were growing up and learning how to be a civilized person. *They* include parents, teachers, relatives, clergy, police, the government, and God as interpreted through the *theys*. Who were your *theys*? What rules did *they* hand down to you, and are you still trying to live by them? Did *they* live by them, or was it "Do as I say and not as I do?"

Karen's father uttered this commandment, "Men don't like women who are too competitive." I met Karen because although she was a wonderful seamstress, she couldn't finish things. There was always a buttonhole that wasn't complete or some threads hanging. Karen adored her father and believed that whatever he told her was the absolute truth. She had to follow his mandate if she wanted to find a man to marry. In her mind, if she finished a sewing project it could be judged excellent and she would be considered a winner. If it wasn't quite finished, it wasn't eligible for judging and she wouldn't be competing.

Procrastinators are not born that way; they are created. The early signs of procrastination often start to develop in child-hood. How many of us loved doing homework or studying for a test? We would much rather have stayed outside playing ball, skating, bike riding or vegging out watching TV. Many high school and college students pull all-nighters since they leave studying and paper writing until the last minute. By the time they graduate, this reaction to the expectations of demanding authorities may become habitual.

As you read on, I will challenge you to free yourself from the chains that bind you to the past in ways that hold you back. As a psychotherapist, I know that it is possible to stop this compulsive behavior once and for all.

What Your Behavior Is Saying

You may be reading this book because you are sick and tired of being sick and tired of the consequences of your procrastination. You may have taken workshops, read books, tried to deal with time better, or even hired a coach, yet you still are late to meetings, still have a pile of unfinished projects waiting on your desk or in your garage and have trouble getting started. That doesn't mean that you are weak or stupid. It means that you haven't gotten to the root of the problem.

All behavior is communication. What does your behavior say about you? Procrastination is a self-sabotaging set of behaviors. If you try to figure out why you do what you do you will come up with a list of flimsy excuses: "I was too tired," "I didn't have the time," "I had to take my kids to the mall," "It was too hot or too cold," or "I had to watch the playoffs."

The real question is not why am I putting this off, it is why do I need to keep myself from going ahead with this? Your list of excuses conceals another level of negative self-talk that a part of you doesn't want to face. Some of the books you have read about overcoming procrastination may have coached you to look at and challenge your negative self-talk. This technique is called Cognitive Therapy. The idea is to substitute another reasonable and true thought for the one you have been harboring.

Once you realize that you have a choice and can create a new and positive way of looking at the situation, you can choose to change your behavior. Sometimes Cognitive Therapy works well, and you are able to change your attitude and your behavior. However, if challenging your thoughts isn't effective and you are still seeking a solution to your procrastination, it means that you haven't gone far enough.

There is yet another layer underneath the level of negative self-talk. I call this layer the "level beyond awareness." This is the unconscious level. The conscious mind is not able to access this hidden area. The information and memories stored in the unconscious have a profound effect on you and you don't even know it. Here you will discover what makes you a procrastinator. Chapter 9 is devoted to helping you uncover these decisions and eradicate the damaging conclusions you chose to believe early in life about yourself and your world that still haunt you.

The Prison of the Mind
It's not what we do that seems to matter, it's what we tell ourselves about what we do that counts. In psychotherapy, we call this a self-fulfilling prophecy. That means that we uncon-

sciously make it come true. Self-fulfilling Prophecies can be either self-affirming or self-critical. Telling yourself "I always lose things," "I'm unlucky in love," "I'm clumsy," will create unhappiness and stress, while believing, " I'm lovable," "I am a good athlete," "I'm an achiever," will encourage a feeling of well being. The more you tell yourself you are a procrastinator, the more you will believe it is the truth, and the more you will make it come true.

Emmet Fox, a wise teacher, wrote a fable about a man who was arrested and put into a dungeon without a trial. In this story, he stayed there, languishing for twenty years. Finally, the prisoner couldn't stand it any longer so he decided to attack the jailer the next day. He hoped the jailer would kill him and put him out of his misery. When he went to the cell door and tried the handle he was shocked to find that the door opened. It had never been locked, but he hadn't known it! "He was a captive, not of stone or iron, but of false belief." He was living in a prison created by his thought.

At the beginning of his incarceration, the prisoner decided that the prison door was locked and acted as if his belief was the truth, but it wasn't. All of us have made decisions from the beginning of our lives and never questioned them. Like the prisoner, we create a life that has its own kind of impenetrable door or bars that keep us in situations that perpetuate our suffering.

Our thoughts and beliefs are so powerful that they create our world. No one can exist without cuts, bruises, illnesses, the loss of loved ones and other forms of pain. It goes with being human. Buddhists believe that pain is unavoidable as we go through life, but suffering is optional. The Psychiatrist, John Diamond, maintains that suffering comes from an accumulation of our negative decisions.

I talk to lots of people, and I listen carefully. Often someone will say something that makes a red warning light go on in my head, because the speaker is assuming that everyone knows that, for instance:

♦ You can't trust men/women because they will always cheat on you.

♦ Politicians are all crooked.

♦ If you can't do something perfectly, there is little point in doing it at all.

Believing these thoughts causes great suffering in my clients' lives. At those times, I feel like Alice in Wonderland talking to the White Queen in *Through the Looking Glass*. When Alice tells the Queen that she can't believe impossible things the Queen replies," I daresay you haven't had much practice... Why, sometimes I've believed as many as six impossible things before breakfast."

Take Action
As you read each chapter, you will be able peel away the layers that contain your excuses and your fearful thoughts to reveal the original negative decisions you made and then forgot that you made. These choices led to your avoidance reactions and encourage your procrastination. In Chapter 4 you will learn a powerful technique called EFT (Emotional Freedom Techniques) to rid yourself of the emotional debris that has been holding you back, allowing you to move forward successfully.

Chapter 3

Getting Started

When I teach a class or workshop about procrastination, I always begin by asking the attendees to choose a goal for practice. The goal is something that they are bothered about putting off. It doesn't have to be something major like deciding to move or get a new job. It can be a task that seems small but is bugging them just the same, like washing the car, making an appointment to get their taxes done, or cleaning off a desk. You will learn a great deal about yourself if you keep your chosen goal in mind as you read each chapter, and work on completing it by using the many exercises you will find.

No two procrastinators act alike. Each one puts off doing things in different areas of their lives. A great many procrastinators have problems meeting deadlines, whether handing in a report on time or paying bills before incurring the penalty. I once had a client named Scott who deferred picking up or opening his mail for so long that he almost lost his house because he didn't pay his mortgage.

I'll Show You!
Scott was depressed because he was having problems at work. He believed that he was being unfairly blamed and

scapegoated for things that he was not responsible for. He always seemed in trouble with his female supervisor. He became very angry with her. Not paying his bills on time, especially his mortgage was his way of thumbing his nose at authority figures. He was the one who suffered because he was acting like a child. In our work together, he realized that he didn't want to grow up, although it was time to behave in an adult manner. After he rescued his home, he began to get caught up on other things that needed fixing there and took in his mail in a timely manner.

Meeting Deadlines

Coming late is a way of missing deadlines. Lateness tends to annoy others more than the latecomer; the ones left standing on the corner, sitting with a cold dinner, or missing the first act of a show. Many people think that coming late is a passive aggressive act, demonstrating unspoken anger. I once polled a class I was teaching and discovered that people who come late do so for many other different reasons. One man said that he felt anxious if he were to go somewhere and was the first person in the room. He wouldn't feel cared for. A woman related that she didn't want to stand out. She might look foolish if she arrived too soon. If others were there before her, she could sneak in unobtrusively.

Some people who have Attention Deficit Disorder are often easily distracted and lose track of time. Perfectionists may have trouble making decisions about what to wear, fearful of not looking perfect, so they put on and take off outfit after outfit and are delayed. In pursuing this issue, I discovered that, like procrastinators, I was also driven by a fear since I am obsessed about having to arrive early to everything. My fear is the fear of missing something important if I am late.

Avoiding Medical Treatment

Procrastination can harm your health too. Doctors notice that some patients don't take their medications after purchasing them. We all know people who won't go to the dentist or see a doctor even though they have symptoms that need attention. Fear can stop people in their tracks despite the negative consequences. Soraya conveniently forgot to make an appointment for her mammogram. Lester wouldn't go for a colon exam, and Russell refused to go near a dentist. Each of them was terrified that they would find out that they had a horrible condition or illness and were angry about their behavior yet refused to face their worries.

Fears of needles, pain, or being seen or touched by strangers can keep people away. In the next chapter I will teach you how to use a simple method called EFT to uncover and release all the anxieties that are standing in your way to achieving good health and energy.

Improving Yourself

Personal improvement projects like losing weight, exercising, meditating, reading self-improvement books, or joining self-help groups fall by the wayside as well. There are even people who avoid having fun! I remember a neighbor who kept avoiding joining a weight loss program and was down on herself. Her devoted husband wanted to buy her a new car, and she refused. When I asked her why, she said, "Fat Frances doesn't deserve to have nice things!" Her belief that she was unworthy kept her from allowing herself to look and feel better and also caused her to push away gifts and love. As you read on you will learn why intelligent people are capable of harming themselves this way even though it apparently doesn't make sense.

Insisting On Perfection

Procrastinators with unreasonably high expectations bear the burden of both their procrastination and their perfectionism. They may have trouble meeting deadlines since the end result may not be good enough. Making decisions is one of the hardest things for perfectionists to do. Many years ago when my children were still in school, I decided to move. I was a single mother with a limited income, but I was fortunate to find a wonderful house near good schools on a pleasant street. It even had a pool. There was only one drawback. The house was directly across the street from the freeway. Cars and trucks were zooming past twenty-four hours a day. I could not make up my mind whether to commit to a mortgage or not since I had to be right –or else!

My perfectionism caused me to become immobilized, so I called ten of my closest friends and relatives for advice. Five of them thought that despite the freeway it was still a good deal while the other five thought I would be crazy to buy it. Time was running out, and I had to make an offer or lose the house. I didn't know what to do. I used the *Worst Case Scenario* technique that you will learn in Chapter 7 and examined my fear. Buying a house meant investing a great deal of money. My worst fear was that I would lose everything. I asked myself if that true. It dawned on me that the worst thing that might happen was that I would live in the house for a while and then sell it to someone else if I was unhappy. I might lose a few thousand dollars, but not everything. I decided to buy the house. Fortunately, it worked out well, and I lived there for ten years.

Perfectionists often worry about how they will look and what people will think about them, their work, their belongings, or even their relatives. This can affect them socially. Consequently, they may come late to engagements or put off mingling with others. There are people who aren't perfectionists who also find excuses for avoiding social situations. They don't want to go to parties or even entertain others. Often it relates to what we call social phobia.

Fear of Eating Out

Amanda was very anxious about attending a barbecue at her daughter's school since eating with others made her very nervous. She usually found excuses for not going to these kinds of outings, however there was no way she could get out of going to this one. You may think this a silly thing to procrastinate about, but all delaying behaviors make sense when you get to know the details of someone's life.

As it turned out, Amanda had been teased and embarrassed by her older siblings at the family dinner table for many years and had developed a fear about being humiliated by strangers while eating with them.

She was not consciously aware that the childhood dinner time abuse was still haunting her so she was amazed to discover what was at the root of her procrastination. She successfully dealt with this phobia by using the secret weapon, EFT that you will learn in the next chapter to eliminate this fear

Now that you have an overview of what procrastination is all about, the different types of behaviors that procrastinators use to dawdle, dally and put off getting started or finishing let's get started with a plan for change. It's simply **One, Two Three, Go!**

One: Your History

Take a few minutes now to think about your behaviors. In what areas of your life do you hold back? Is it at work more than in your private life or vice versa? Do you come late to work or appointments? Do you have trouble with deadlines, making decisions, socializing, or taking care of yourself physically, emotionally or spiritually?

The origins of procrastination frequently begin in childhood. Can you remember when you started to act this way? How old you were when you first started to avoid things? What was going on in your life? Were there unhappy things happening at home? Was school involved? What were you telling yourself about your life? If there were stresses, how did you handle them?

Pat recalled that she began to dawdle as a small child with five siblings. At times she felt overwhelmed among so many. Procrastinating got her attention and made her feel special, although it was negative attention. Unfortunately, she is still doing it thirty years later.

Before you read further please make a mental note of what, at this moment, is still waiting to be done. What have you started but not finished? Perhaps you painted the kitchen but haven't put the curtains back up. Have you pulled the weeds on your front lawn, but haven't gotten around to doing the same in the back yard? Think about things you haven't begun that have deadlines and need to be taken care of like paying bills, sending a birthday card or responding to an invitation that demands an RSVP. Is there anything else that you are annoyed at yourself for not working on? Maybe you have two years' worth of magazines you haven't read yet, or you bought tiles to decorate the back splash in the kitchen, but they are still in unopened cartons in the garage. Choose one of these as the goal you are committing yourself to complete while reading this book.

Two: Get Smart
One reason procrastinators fail is that they may not know how to set a smart goal at the start. You won't succeed unless your goal is specific and concrete. Chelsea, one of my students, said that her goal was to fix up her bedroom. What does "fix up"

mean? Is she going to paint it, get new furniture, pick up her clothes, or all of these? If Chelsea says that she is going to paint the walls, buy a new bed and a new spread, she knows what her goal is.

When you decide to lose weight, exercise, or read to improve your mind, you need to be clear about your expectations. Determine how many pounds you want to lose to be successful, how many days you are going to exercise and for how long, and how many books you'll read in order to congratulate yourself for following through. If you don't have a clear goal you won't know when you have completed it.

Sometimes we overestimate our ability to reach a goal. I once taught a weight control class that met for eight weeks. Most people can usually lose two pounds a week when they are committed. Lori, set a goal of losing twenty pounds in that time despite my warning about setting herself up for disappointment. At the last class, when others were smiling at reaching their goals of losing ten to fifteen pounds, Lori was sobbing. She felt like a failure because she had only lost eighteen pounds although that was more than anyone else in the class!

Maybe you have chosen a goal that is specific and attainable, but when you think of working on it, you cringe at the idea of getting started or completing it. It may feel too harsh or unreasonable and unfair. When you choose a target because you think you *should*, it most likely means that it is someone else's desire for you. Ted insisted that biking ten miles a day, seven days a week was a smart goal, but he had a full time job and was attending school at night. The unrealistic expectation set him up for failure.

Finally, ask yourself if this is a good time to achieve your goal. Lana's objective was to take a class in creative writing. The goal was specific, attainable, and reasonable, but her in-laws were coming to stay for a month. She wouldn't have time to complete the goal with visitors in her life and her home and would most likely feel like a failure for dropping out when her life became complicated with entertaining her guests.

Re-examine the goal you have just decided to complete. Is it smart? If you are not sure, talk your plan over with a friend you trust to give you good feedback to make sure you are setting off on the right track.

Three: Eliminate Excuses
You may be feeling a lot of pressure in your life to achieve a variety of goals, meet deadlines and have something to show for your efforts. At the end of the day you want to relax, yet often more chores await you as well as family obligations. Do *should's, oughts, musts* and *have to's* control you? Are you using excuses to condone putting things off to avoid guilt or shame for not living up to the expectations of others?

Excuses act as a smokescreen that keeps you from understanding what your behavior is really all about. You have just thought about your unfinished tasks and projects. You have choosen one in particular to work on while you read this book. Now I want you to list all the excuses you might give yourself and others for delaying. We all play the game of giving alleged reasons for procrastinating and accepting each other's justifications. Everyone we know does this, friends, family, co-workers and even the government. Reasons and rationalizations come easily. Have you ever noticed how inventive we are in our ability to create explanations for postponing? I have been compiling a list for over twenty years and have discovered that excuses fall into different categories.

Words justifying inaction because of time constraints slip trippingly off the tongue of many dawdlers. "I'll do it later," "I can do it another time," "I don't have enough time to do it all," "I still have time before the deadline," or its cousin, "Ninety percent is done. It can wait a little longer." are variations on this theme. Another modification is "I'll do it now... but first I'll make dinner, watch the World Series, finish this chapter, take a nap etc." Don't forget the universal dieter's put-off, "I'll start on Monday."

The pretext that there is a physical problem holding up completion of the waiting project sounds like this: "I'm tired;" "I've been working hard, and I deserve a break;" or "I'll stay up too late and miss my sleep." Kitty suggested that her biorhythms were out of whack and Max maintained that his doctor said that he should go exercise instead. A New Age student explained, "My horoscope shows that it's not auspicious because Mercury is retrograde." Who can argue with that?

Some excuses blame someone or something else for your inability to take action. Jack maintained that there is no doubt that he would have completed the task last week if only he had the right equipment while his neighbor, Bob had to wait for a sale so he could get the parts cheaper. It is easy to absolve yourself if you have to check with someone and wait until he is available, and you are definitely in the clear when you know that others won't cooperate. When in doubt, a seasoned procrastinator can come up with a generic reason, "It's too hot, too cold, too early, too late, too boring, or too costly." Another justification is blaming your house for not having enough room to store all the supplies you will need.

My heart goes out to the procrastinators whose excuses ring of compassion or good citizenship. During a drought year one upstanding homeowner who procrastinated about watering his lawn announced, "I'm saving water." Another frugal procrastinator felt righteous because putting off a project would save energy costs. A college student in one of my workshops whined, "I've got a new girlfriend and I have to give her time."

Your excuses may be a clue to your psychological state of mind. The excuse, "I'm not in the mood," may reveal depression. The compulsive spender's excuse for putting things off is, "Nordstrom's was having a sale and I had to go." Marriage counseling might be in order for the passive aggressive wife who was slyly getting back at her spouse when she declared, "If I don't do it my husband will."

Then there's the philosophical existential "Why change!" or "The concept of time is a mere construct." I have heard excuses that run the gamut from prosaic to poetic, but my favorite was tossed off by a young man who may have been a student of Buddhism, someone who is truly living in the now, when he said, "I'm young — there's time."

Now that I've shared my long list with you, I'm going to ask you to review your own list of excuses. You may want to add some from the list above. Read them to yourself. Draw a dark line through all of them because from now on we will consider them worthless. They won't get you off the hook anymore.

Go!
Excuses are the tip of the iceberg of procrastination, the part that sticks out above the expanse of the unconscious mind. Excuses keep you from understanding what procrastination is really all about. Excuses keep you stuck in avoidance. Now that they are out of the way, you can turn to the real core issues that lie beneath your delay tactics and free yourself once and for all.

24

--

Chapter 4

EFT: The Secret Weapon

Imagine having a process to motivate yourself to stop procrastinating that is easy to do. What if you could get to the heart of what is keeping you stuck and find solutions to your delaying behavior without struggling with frustration and guilt? You can do all this and more with EFT (Emotional Freedom Techniques). You can learn it in minutes and use it anytime and anywhere.

EFT is a new method that is based on ancient wisdom. Five thousand years ago, the Chinese discovered energy pathways in the body called meridians and numerous energy points that exist along them. We know that these points actually exist because we can measure the electrical resistance on the skin and compare the measurement at acupuncture points with non-acupuncture points. There is a definite difference. When we tap or rub these points, it is called acupressure.

EFT is acupressure for the emotions. Simply tap or gently rub on only eight energy points to balance the body's energy field and achieve effective results. Tapping certain points causes the serotonin, a chemical in your brain, to rise and reduce stress. As the system becomes more balanced, negative thoughts and memories that contribute to the urge to procrastinate diminish or disappear.

The diagram below shows the eight energy points that you will need to tap or rub using a very light touch. To do this, use two fingers --- your index and middle fingers held together. Start with the Karate Chop spot. Tap each spot gently for about 3 seconds. If you feel sore, it may mean you are tapping too vigorously. If you have a problem tapping on your face or hands due to arthritis or another type of sensitivity, you may touch or rub the spots using very little pressure.

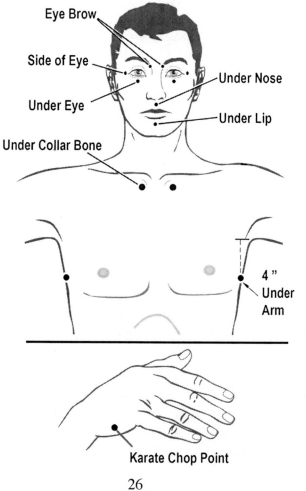

Get Ready

Beginning Point: Always begin with the Karate Chop Spot:

♦ *The Karate Chop Spot.* This is the area along the outside edge of your hand below your little finger.

Although you do not need to stimulate the remaining points in any specific order, most people find that going from top to bottom is the easiest way to remember them.

Remaining Points

♦ *Eyebrow* is where the hair of your eyebrow begins near the nose.

♦ *Outside corner of the eye* is on the bone at the outer corner of your eye socket.

♦ *Under the eye* is right under the lower lid at the middle of the eye above the cheekbone.

♦ *Under the nose* is between the bottom of the nose and the upper lip.

♦ *Under the lower lip* is in the indentation below your lower lip.

♦ *Under the collarbone* is one inch under the knob of your collarbone about one inch off the center of your breastbone

♦ *Under the arm* is four inches below the armpit on the side of your body.

Practice tapping gently on these points until you know them by heart.

You can use either hand or both hands at the same time. You may tap the points on one side of your body, alternate sides, tap both sides simultaneously, or tap both sides alternating right and left. Find the way you like best.

Now that you are familiar with the energy points and know how to stimulate them, you are ready to apply EFT to overcome your procrastination problem. It is as easy as Five Simple Steps.

Five Easy Steps

Step One: Choose a situation, problem, negative emotion or physical sensation that you want to eliminate or resolve. You might focus on something you are avoiding starting, something that you can't seem to finish, or the thought that it won't be good enough.

Step Two: Rate the intensity of your emotions or negative energy on a scale from zero to ten with ten being extremely intense/upset/angry/anxious and zero meaning neutral and free of discomfort.

Step Three: Create a focusing statement and say it out loud or to yourself three times as you tap your Karate Chop Spot on the edge of your hand. The focusing statement names the problem or emotion that needs changing followed by a positive statement. For example: "Even though I keep putting off starting this project, I am a good person at heart." "Even though I took a nap when I should have been washing the car, I am ready to release my procrastination now." "Even though I can't get myself to clean off my desk, I am tapping on that now."

Step Four: Follow the tapping sequence on the remaining energy points while you use a reminder phrase about the issue or feeling you are treating. At each point you can say or think a word or phrase like "procrastination," " I can't get going," or "messy desk."

Step Five: Take a deep breath, let it out, and take stock of how you feel now. Rate yourself again. Are you as upset/anxious

28

--

angry as when you started? Did any memories, thoughts or ideas spring to mind? Start with Step One and tap about the new thoughts, feelings or memories. If nothing new comes to mind, keep tapping about the original issue.

Repeat Steps One through Five until you have discovered a solution to your problem or until the negative feeling is gone. Although you will find that you can perform a round of tapping in one minute once you are familiar with the system, let me explain each step in greater detail to make it easier for you to succeed.

Helpful Hints

There is no right or wrong way to use EFT. You will find that tapping can eliminate the urge to put things off. You can tap when you realize that you are using the excuse to go shopping instead of working on a report or phoning your mother. When you have a headache or upset stomach, you most likely will reach for an aspirin or antacid to relieve the symptom. With EFT you don't have to wait until you feel the urge to procrastinate. You can treat your compulsion to put things off simply by thinking about how you usually put things off, the last time you put something off, how you may find excuses for procrastinating now or about the problem in general.

A treatment can be one or two rounds of EFT lasting for a few minutes or longer. When you want to eliminate negative emotions like fear, anxiety and anger about a specific incident, one treatment may resolve it. You may feel relief in one minute, after just one or two rounds. Complicated issues may bring up memories or new thoughts and take longer to resolve. Sometimes you may tap a few times a day or tap daily for a week or more. If you are not noticing change after two weeks you might want to consult a psychotherapist or EFT practitioner to help you move past the block.

You will find that you have better results when you pick a specific aspect of your problem. Start with one of these.

♦ When you catch yourself procrastinating
♦ When you are angry with yourself because you are not doing what you are supposed to do
♦ When you feel guilt and shame about the results of putting things off
♦ When you feel anger towards those who are demanding that you complete tasks
♦ When you recall memories of the negative consequences you have endured because you procrastinated

The Rating System

When you think about the situation or feeling that you want to treat ask yourself how upset you feel *right now*. Perhaps you were angrier or more fearful a while ago, but *now* is what is important. Do your best to estimate how much negative energy you feel or how intense the urge is to sidetrack yourself.

If the idea of picking a number from one to ten daunts you, consider whether the intensity of the negative charge is *a little, a moderate amount or a great deal*. This is just a guide to help you see that you are letting go of the problem. Sometimes when people reach zero they can't remember how upset they were at the beginning. Keeping track of the change in the numbers will prove to you that EFT is working. If you can't get in touch with an emotional response, it is fine to think about the situation without rating it and go on to Step Three.

The Focusing Statement

The focusing statement consists of two parts: naming the

problem and focusing on a positive thought. It will sound like this. "Even though I have this problem, I deeply and completely accept myself." Although it may seem as if you are dwelling on the negative when you say, "Even though I have this problem," you are simply pinpointing the troubled area that needs treatment. You might think of it as tuning in to a radio station. Chapter 6 will explain more about how the brain works and why you need to focus on your problem in order to achieve lasting results.

If you can't say, "I completely accept myself," or "I am a good person at heart," think up something else that you can accept that is positive. Most people are willing to affirm, "I am doing the best I can right now." Positive statements generate positive energy that can aid healing. Some others that my clients use are,

♦ I am giving myself a treatment for this now.
♦ I am tapping on this now.
♦ I am exploring this now.
♦ I am ready to release all of this now.
♦ I am letting go of this now.
♦ It's over and I am OK.

Streamlined focusing statements are short and simple. Here are some examples.
♦ Even though I can't control my procrastination, I love and accept myself.
♦ Even though I went to the beach instead of working on my paper, I am doing my best to stop procrastinating.
♦ Even though I got angry with my husband for nagging at me and dragged my feet so we were late, I am a good human being.
♦ Even though I hate myself for not handing in my report on time, God loves me.

Creating an expanded focusing statement in which you explain more about the situation and talk our loud to yourself may be very beneficial. Use your own words for the best effect. Remember that you can say anything you want and even use curse words if it is fitting since no one is listening.

Remember to tap your Karate Chop Spot while you are saying your focusing statement three times.

- Even though I waited until the last minute to find the perfect present for my sister and didn't get it to her until a month after her birthday, and I can't understand why she still wants to be my friend since I treat her like this, I am treating myself for doing this kind of thing again and again.
- Even though I have to pay a late fee on my credit card again, and I hate myself for being so lazy, I am ready to be rid of this habit.
- Even though I promised the customer that I would be finished landscaping his yard by the end of the month and wasn't finished. Even though the customer was angry with me and threatened to tell others that I am unreliable, I am ready to stop doing this to others and myself.

Keep Focused

After you say your version of the focusing statement, "Even though I have this problem, I am tapping on it now," tap each of the remaining energy points quickly five to ten times or gently hold for 3 seconds while you concentrate on your problem or the negative emotional state you want to heal. You can do this in your mind or out loud. As you do this, say or think a shortened reminder phrase. You don't have to say, "Even though I have this problem." You only need to say a word or short phrase because you already know what you are tapping about. It is not necessary to repeat the entire statement.

If you are focusing on your predilection for coming late all the time, the set-up statement might be, "Even though I tend to come late all the time, I am doing my best to eliminate this problem." The reminder phrase might be, "late." "coming late," "can't stop coming late," or "problem of lateness."

You may have different feelings and responses every time you tap. Some of the common reactions to EFT are relaxation, feeling energy in your body, sighing, giggling, sadness, anger, crying, remembering, understanding, release, and relief. Sometimes people don't get the result they expect because they are holding back and repressing their emotions or thoughts, even though no one is there to hear it.

At times, it helps to use a longer reminder phrase.

Say It Like It Is!
Emily remembered something terrible that her mother did to her when she was six that was very painful, and she tried to make light of it. I suggested that in order to get the best result she needed to say exactly how she really felt as the reminder phrase, "How could you have done that to me! You hurt me so much and you weren't even sorry!" Only after she allowed herself to acknowledge those feelings was she able to let it go and truly experience the understanding, "It's over. I survived, and I am OK today."

Say whatever has meaning for you. Sometimes you may want to grunt, make a loud noise or scream to express how you feel. That is fine. If you have a lump in your throat or butterflies in your stomach, you don't need to use words. Simply focus on the sensation as you tap. If it moves around from your throat to your chest, focus on your chest for the next round. Keep following the body's responses until they are all gone.

What Did You Notice?

When you have finished a round of tapping, be sure to take a deep breath and let it out. At that point, I always ask my clients, "What did you notice?" At first you may be so intent on doing the tapping correctly and hitting all the points that you don't notice much. There are two kinds of outcomes to a round of EFT. You will either notice that your level of discomfort lessens on the scale of zero to ten and you feel more relaxed or you experience different emotions, thoughts, memories or answers. You may even undergo both simultaneously.

If you are aware that you started your focusing statement feeling frustrated with a rating of nine and now you feel frustrated with a level of four, begin again and see if the level continues to decline. Change the wording of your reminder phrase to reflect the changes. If you started by saying, "Even though I am so frustrated with myself because I waited until the last minute to buy a new water heater that was on sale, and the stores were closed when I got there, so I had to pay full price that was $50 more when I finally got around to it," change to, "Even though I am less upset with myself now, I am continuing to tap on what happened."

Keep doing this until you are at zero, feeling no trace of frustration/anxiety/sadness. Then perform this test. Force yourself to think about the problem you started with or try to bring back the frustration, anger, fear, etc. If you still feel some kind of negative emotion keep tapping until it is totally gone. If you are at zero and remain at zero you are finished.

Twigs and Branches

When you find as you tap that you have new thoughts, feelings or memories, or your level of upset goes up instead of down, it means that something else is coming into your consciousness. These are called *aspects*. An *aspect* represents a facet that

34

--

is contributing to the problem. Imagine that a tree trunk symbolizes your problem. The aspects are the twigs and branches on that tree. They are like pieces in a puzzle. As you collect each piece and put them together the greater picture materializes.

It is common for people who tap while feeling great anger to have it suddenly transform into sadness. Tap the next round feeling the sadness to see where that leads. Perhaps you are tapping about your husband or wife and a memory about your father appears. In the next round, use EFT for this new father memory. Whatever comes up next is what you tap in the following round. Any time you feel stuck simply return to the original problem you started with.

Diabetic's Dilemma

Priscilla, an overweight thirty year-old diabetic, put off dieting and ate the wrong foods. She said that she wanted to be healthy and kept buying foods that would keep her sugar level in balance, however she tended to eat more sweets than she should, and often most of the healthy food rotted in her refrigerator. Her poor food choices kept her from shedding pounds.

After just a few minutes of EFT, Priscilla uncovered why she did this. If she followed through, stopped eating sweets and ate the healthy foods she would become healthier and slimmer. Then she wouldn't have an excuse for not socializing. Next, Priscilla got in touch with a secret fear that diabetics die young. She was afraid that if she met someone and fell in love, he would reject her because she was diabetic. These fears felt very real to her as they came into her conscious mind.

She practiced EFT about her worries of the future. It wasn't

about healthy food to begin with. It was about fears of
rejection in the future. EFT helped Priscilla realize that she
deserved to be healthy. With proper eating and treatment she
could live a long life. She soon began to change her eating
habits.

As you tap, specific feelings of fear, anxiety, anger, guilt, or
shame will disappear. Sad or frightening memories will no
longer affect you. They will become neutralized. You will
see problems in a new light and find new solutions that feel
appropriate. Remember to try to bring back the feeling when
you reach zero. If you were working to heal an old memory,
play the memory in your imagination as if you are watching
a movie. Stop whenever you feel emotional and tap until that
scene is neutral. Keep doing this until you can watch the story
straight through without any negative reaction. Here is another
example.

Christopher Grows Up

Christopher was at his wits' end. He reported that he spent
too much time at his computer or doing puzzles, listening to
his iPod or sleeping the morning away. It sounded to me like
a strong need to avoid something, but avoid what? He was
a forty-year-old man who had moved back into his parents'
home after losing his job. It wasn't working out so his parents
asked him to move out as soon as possible, but he was
dawdling looking for apartments. He wasn't happy and they
weren't happy, so why was he procrastinating?

As he tapped on his behavior he got in touch with his
excuses, "I don't know where I want to live." and "Can I find
something I can afford? " Then a few more rounds brought
up the thought, "I always get pushed along by others, and
I don't get the chance to decide what *I* want, so I never

accomplish anything significant in my life." Christopher told me that in his teens he was very rebellious and was kicked out of school. His parents didn't know how to handle him and made him leave the house. He felt as if he didn't have any control over his life. Now his parents were doing it again.

More tapping revealed that the deeper reason for delaying was a feeling of rebelling against his parents for trying to push him out again the way they had in his teen years. It was all about who was in control. He tapped and reported, "This control thing has pervaded my whole life, money problems, relationships with women I wanted who didn't want me, and my work life too." Christopher had lived his life as if he was a ship without a rudder being swept along without any clear destinations.

As he continued to use EFT he came to the conclusion that it wasn't all his parents' fault. He also recognized that he was no longer a teenager and was in charge of his own life. No one was controlling him anymore. He decided to start apartment hunting without anger and became more excited about having his own place and privacy to do what he wanted without his parents treating him like a child again.

Procrastination is a complex problem. Use EFT whenever necessary as new situations come up that trigger your desire to postpone or distract yourself from an undertaking. Treat yourself once or many times a day depending on what you are noticing.

Preventive Tapping

You can use EFT before you even think of procrastinating. Suppose that you are given an assignment at work, or have promised yourself or spouse that you will do a chore at home.

Before you have the chance to think that it is too hot today, that you don't have the right tools, or that it's OK to spend some time at the computer or visit a friend instead, stop and take a deep breath. Then use EFT saying,

♦ Even though I have taken on this project, I know that I usually find excuses for putting it off, so I am giving myself a preventive treatment.

♦ Even though I most likely will not jump into this project immediately but will find ways to distract myself, I am exploring my behavior now to understand what makes me tick.

Then tap the remaining points using a reminder phrase like, "Urge to put it off," "Don't want to do it," or "Distract myself."

Using EFT for two minutes as you start your day takes the edge off your stress. I call this "weed whacking." Don't feed your emotional weeds. Nip them in the bud with daily tapping. The more you tap, the more you will remember to tap. You don't have to sweat the urge to delay-- just tap it away.

Resistance to Change

Human beings are very complex. We often turn away from our good and find excuses for hanging on to our misery. Before you go any further in this book, I recommend that you treat yourself for any possible hidden resistance to letting go of your procrastination or perfectionistic thinking. Here are ten hidden beliefs buried below the surface of your conscious mind that may block your success and sabotage your best efforts.

Blocking Beliefs

♦ I don't deserve to get over this problem.

♦ God is punishing me.

- I will never get over this problem.
- If I get over this problem, I won't be safe.
- I'm not sure I want to get over this problem.
- If I get over this problem, I will lose my identity.
- If I get over this problem, it will be bad for someone else.
- It is impossible to get over this problem.
- I don't have the strength or will power to get over this problem.
- My stuckness can only be solved by someone else.

Show Me That You Love Me

Barry made very little money, couldn't afford his own apartment, and had to rent a room in someone's home, but he kept putting off looking for a job that paid more. His excuse for not job hunting was that he didn't have enough energy after working the long hours he had to work to make ends meet. He had put himself into a double bind, and it seemed impossible to get free. What he didn't know was that unconsciously he *wasn't sure that he wanted to get over his problem* with procrastination. It turned out that if he took power over his life and was more successful he would *lose his identity* as a victim.

Barry's early years were filled with horrible abuse. He was still furious at being injured by both his parents and wanted his dad to make restitution, but his father was cold and distant. Using EFT, Barry explored his situation and frustration about procrastinating. He discovered an irrational belief that was holding him back: *Money is love.* He said, "If I am powerless enough my dad will take care of me and give me money to make my life easier. If he gives me money it means he loves me." In order to get love, Barry had to remain a financially needy victim who needed rescuing. Meanwhile, his father couldn't' care less that he was miserable. The only one really suffering was Barry. As he tapped, he decided that he wanted to stop living life that way. Recently he was able to move into his own place in a beautiful neighborhood.

A Deadly Sin

Maryanne wanted to join a gym to help her lose weight but kept putting off signing up. Meanwhile she vilified herself whenever she overate and kept binging. During one of our sessions, she blurted out that God was punishing her for her gluttony. Since she viewed herself as a sinner, she thought that her punishment was to stay fat and feel guilty. When she tapped, she was able to challenge this belief in light of her other beliefs that God is love and she was a child of God.

As you think about some of the things you are putting off doing now, refer to the list of blocking beliefs and notice which ones have a negative charge. Use EFT to explore it. Pick one of the suggestions from the following list or create your own. Tap on your Karate Chop Spot and say it. Then say a reminder phrase as you tap the remaining points three times around and see what happens. Take stock, and if you are not at zero, keep tapping until you feel as if you have explored this thoroughly and it is no longer true for you.

- ♦ Even though I have some blocks to clearing up my procrastination problem, I am tapping about that now.

- ♦ Even though I am extremely stubborn and don't really want to get over it, I am exploring that idea now.

- ♦ Even though I would lose my identity if I stop procrastinating, I am doing the best I can.

- Even though I'll never get over procrastinating, I am tapping anyway.

- Even though I'm not ready to get over procrastinating, I am a loving and kind person.

- Even though I rationalize that there are some advantages to procrastinating, I deeply and completely accept myself.

Variations

Once you become familiar with the Five Easy Steps approach you can explore some of these variations. If you are at work and need to give yourself a treatment but worry about looking strange in front of co-workers, take a quiet moment and just imagine your fingers touching each energy point and going "tap, tap, tap." You will be pleasantly surprised to find that you get the same results as when you actually tap with your fingers.

When you have a specific problem that you feel unable to resolve, I recommend that you use a variation I call *Be Your Own Best Friend*. Pretend that you are on the phone telling your best friend about this troubling situation. As you tap each energy point, say something new about what's bothering you. Keep going round and round, tapping all the points and talking continuously. After a few minutes, you will notice that you begin to have new thoughts or feelings. As you become calmer, you will feel a shift in your energy and will be able to see the situation from a different viewpoint and make new decisions. Keep talking until you feel pleased with your conclusions.

Be Your Own Best Friend
George tried the *Be Your Own Best Friend* technique because he couldn't bring himself to clean out his storage closet and couldn't figure out why, since it was not a difficult job.

Although he had been divorced for five years, and his ex-wife had remarried, he still had boxes with some of her belongings in that closet. First, he tapped his Karate Chop Spot and said, "Even though I keep putting off cleaning out the storage closet, I am exploring my procrastination now." Then he kept talking as he tapped the other points. It sounded like this:

♦ Eyebrow: I can't imagine why I am not organizing that closet.

♦ Side of eye: It's a chore.

♦ Under lower lid: Some of Jane's things are still there and I should get rid of them.

♦ Under nose: I hate doing it alone.

♦ Under lower lip: There's not really a lot to do. I could finish it in one afternoon.

♦ Under collarbone: I feel angry and resentful when I think of that.

♦ Under arm: Doing it alone.

♦ Eyebrow: No one is helping me or taking care of me.

♦ Side of eye: Jane used to do these things.

♦ Under lower lid: She made a home for me and took care of me.

♦ Under nose: But she left and I am all alone.

♦ Under lower lip: I secretly hoped she would come back.

♦ Under collarbone: I feel so sad and alone.

♦ Under arm: very sad.

♦ He tapped three rounds while feeling intense sadness, saying, "I will be alone forever."

♦ Eyebrow: Jane is gone.

♦ Side of eye: She didn't want me.

- ♦ Under lower lid: Who will want me now?
- ♦ Under nose: Maybe it's not too late for me.
- ♦ Under lower lip: Maybe I can find someone else to love.
- ♦ Under collarbone: Why not!
- ♦ Under arm: I can do it!

George let go of his fantasy that Jane might return, cleaned out his closet and went on with a more positive attitude toward his social life.

Tapping Practice

Now that you have read the instructions for using EFT, here are some situations to tap about.

- ♦ When I put off working on/ starting to work on / or finishing _____ I use the excuse _____to let myself off the hook.

- ♦ If I complete _____ I am worried that _____ will happen, and I couldn't live that down.

- ♦ Every time I try to be on time, I seem to sabotage myself.

- ♦ I remember what happened the last time I procrastinated about _____,

Muscle Test to Check it Out

Sometimes when you test yourself by trying to go back to the original feeling, memory or thought and find that you seem calm and untroubled, there may still be more work to do. I have treated clients who felt fine after working with EFT, but had new upsetting memories or emotions emerge during the following week and told themselves, "EFT doesn't work." They

43
--

were unaware of the process that clearing out one layer of
issues may reveal another unexamined one. Sometimes deeper
layers lie in the unconscious. I will tell you about implicit
memories that are held in the body without words in Chapter 6.

There are a few ways that you can ask your unconscious
questions that your conscious mind may not be able to answer.
One of these, Muscle Testing, is derived from kinesiology and
is often used by chiropractors and some doctors. The body can
answer questions with a yes or no when pressure is applied to
certain muscles. They either stay strong or go weak. You can
easily learn to do this for yourself. Experiment with each of
these processes and see which one works best for you.

Open the Ring

Put the tips of your thumb and ring finger or little finger of
your non-dominant hand together. Use the index finger of
your dominant hand as a wand and place it inside the space
made by your fingers. Say, "I am male." Then try to break the
fingers apart with your index finger by moving it outward.
Notice if the fingers come apart easily or stay together. Make
sure that you wait until you have completed the statement
before moving the index finger. Now say, "I am female," and
do the same thing. Usually the fingers will remain together if
the statement is true and easily come apart for false, although
some people find that the opposite occurs. Test this by saying
some other true or false statements like, "Two plus two equals
four, Two plus two equals seven," or "Today is Monday, Today
is Saturday." Your fingers should hold each time you utter a
true statement and open without a great deal of pressure if the
answer is false.

Figure Eight

Another simple way to muscle test yourself is to make a circle by pressing the thumb and index fingers of each hand together and then putting one set of fingers inside the other to form a figure eight chain. This time, say one of the true/false statements aloud and then try to pull the fingers apart. If they hold it usually means yes or true. Try this a few times with whatever questions you already know the answers to and make sure you always get the same result for yes and no.

Stand and Sway

When people have trouble with the finger testing, or if you have arthritis or other problems with you hands, the stand and sway method may be the best for you. Stand with your feet firmly on the floor. Remove any high-heeled shoes if necessary. Let your arms hang loosely at your side and take a few deep breaths. Say one of the yes/no statements and watch what you body does. It may sway forward for yes and backward for no. Some people sway toward one side or the other. I have seen a few people who stand stock still for no and sway for yes. Again, try saying these statements until you get the same results each time the answer is yes/ true or no/false.

Your Fingers Know

While you are seated comfortably in an armchair, you can explore this relaxation technique called ideomotor signaling. Put your arms on the arms of the chair with your hands gently resting, palms down with fingers relaxed. Tell your body to indicate which finger is the yes finger and which the no finger when you say the true/false statement. The finger may tingle, quiver, or even rise up. The yes or no finger can be on either hand or the same hand. Say the statements out loud, then be still and notice what your fingers tell you.

Pendulum Fun

If you still haven't found the way to ask your Inner Self questions, consider using a pendulum. You can make your own by tying a key to a piece of string or yarn, using a locket or heavy bead on a chain or string, or something else like that. Sit comfortably in an armchair. Hold the string of your pendulum lightly with your thumb and forefinger and let it swing freely. Rest your elbow on the arm of the chair to support your arm. Pendulums are fun to use because they can swing in many ways: around in circles to the left or the right, toward you and away from you, and left to right and back again. As you have done before, say the yes/no statement and watch what the pendulum does each time. Notice what direction it swings for yes and no. or true or false Occasionally a person will find that for either the yes or the no answer, the pendulum stands perfectly still.

Once you know how to tell when an answer is true or false, you can use one or more of these procedures to ask questions to which you don't know the answer. You will find that it comes in handy when you need to know:

♦ Am I finished with this problem?

♦ How many issues must I address to clear this fear/anger/ scary memory? (Ask each of these separately: One? More than one? Less than five? Etc.)

♦ Do I have to tap on each issue separately?

♦ Can I clear all the issues related to this problem simultaneously?

♦ How young was I when I developed this fear? (Ask each of these separately: Pre birth? Infancy? Less than five? Less than ten? Etc.)

♦ Is EFT the best way to treat myself for this problem?

The more you examine yourself inside and out with the help of your Inner Wisdom and energy tapping, the more you will realize that EFT is a remarkable system for helping you overcome putting things off. When you find a few minutes a day to use EFT, you will reap benefits that will change your life.

Chapter 5

Thinking Doesn't Make It So

When Theresa was fifty she divorced her husband of thirty years. She had been a homemaker all that time and hadn't worked. Because he was no longer supporting her, she had to find a job. She would get up every morning with the intention of looking for work, but would find so many distractions that she never got around to following through. When she consulted me about her problem she remarked, "I am too old and fat. I am embarrassed to go for an interview. No one will want to hire me." Her beliefs kept her sitting at home feeling depressed and stuck.

I once knew an inspirational minister who said, "The Truth with a capital T is true for everyone, everywhere, all the time. If it isn't, then it is just your opinion. And you can change your opinion." Theresa believed what she told me with all her heart. If the scenario she described were guaranteed to happen, I wouldn't blame her for not wanting to go to interviews. Was it the Truth with a capital T? Is it true that all overweight fifty-year-olds are turned down for jobs? When Theresa spoke to me, I had no doubt that her tale of woe was just her opinion.

Distorted Thinking

People who are members of twelve step groups often talk about
how their *Stinkin' Thinkin'* leads them to relapse. *Stinkin'
Thinkin'* is what Dr. David Burns, well known psychiatrist
and author terms cognitive distortions. That means that your
thinking is twisted. In other words, you believe your opinions
are the Truth with a capital T. According to Dr. Burns, when
you feel the way you think and your thinking is negative, you
put yourself into a depressed state. That sums up what *Stinkin'
Thinkin'* is all about.

At times, just being aware of your *Stinkin' Thinkin'* is enough
to change your attitude, however if not you can use EFT to
re-evaluate whether it is the truth. Here are four examples of
distortions we are all guilty of and how EFT can help you deal
with them.

All or Nothing

One of the most harmful kinds of distortion is *All or Nothing*
thinking. If you have only two choices, all or nothing, good or
bad, black or white, perfect or failure, you will paint yourself
into a corner. This is especially true of perfect or failure. When
you have to earn an A or you consider yourself a failure, you
don't leave room to feel OK with a B plus or A minus. I have
counseled many college students who procrastinate about
handing in papers or even taking classes where they might not
excel. I tell them that, although I was very much like them when
I was in college, since I graduated no one has ever asked me
what grade I got in Freshman English, Philosophy, History of
Art, or any other class I took. They only wanted to know that
I got my degree! I wish that I had had someone to help prevent
me from carrying my own twisted thinking to such a degree
that I dropped out of graduate school (as I described to you at
the start of this book).

EFT can help you get out of the trap of *All or Nothing* thinking. Perfectionists are especially liable to judge themselves by the *perfect or failure* principle.

You're Never Too Old To Change

Jacob at 70 was long retired. His wife had also recently retired and was getting a lot of mail about her pension and her 401K. Jacob was an early riser and greeted the mail carrier delivering the mail first thing in the morning. He would take it into the kitchen, sit at the table and look through the envelopes.

Whenever he saw something that looked "technical" he would put it aside. When the pile in the kitchen grew too big Jacob would transfer it to the basket on the wet bar in the family room, and when that basket was overflowing the unopened mail landed in a box in the hall closet because he couldn't bring himself to look at the growing piles.

By the time I met Jacob he was filled with self-loathing and frustration. After all, a man his age should know about stock proxies and pensions. He was so frightened of handling his wife's business affairs incorrectly that he would not even open the envelopes that contained the words he was afraid he wouldn't understand. He had to do it right or else, a clear example of *all or nothing* thinking.

When Jacob began to tap he said, "Even though I can't make myself open all the mail, and I keep putting it off so it is now totally unmanageable, I am doing the best I can." As he tapped, this is what he said after each round.

♦ I remember being in the second grade in Catholic School.

♦ I can still see Sister Ann standing in front of the class.

- She was very mean.

- She would punish us if we gave the wrong answer.

- I was scared. I can still see her eyes looking at me.

- I was afraid to get it wrong.

- That's how I feel when I am sitting at the kitchen table all alone in the morning with the mail.

- I can see her standing in front of me.

- I can feel that fear in my throat.

- He feels the fear as he taps.

- But I am not seven. I am seventy!

- She is just a memory from my past.

- He laughs. What a surprise that something like that is still affecting me.

Jacob freed himself from the ghost of Sister Ann and realized that he could find out the meaning of the words in the letters and ask his wife to join him so they could deal with her retirement business together.

Crystal Ball Gazing

This distortion in thinking happens when you think you can predict the future. Tim had trouble buying gifts for people since he thought he should be able to read their minds. He usually told himself that his gift wouldn't be right and convinced himself that the recipient wouldn't like whatever he chose. When you think you know what the future will bring, and it is a negative prediction, you are setting yourself up to procrastinate in order to avoid your prophecy from coming to pass. This is Crystal Ball Gazing. You fill your head with calamitous visions that you assume will happen.

The Gift Giving Quandry

Tim waited until two days before Christmas to send his brother a gift because he couldn't come up with something perfect. Then, at the last minute, he ordered something online that wasn't perfect, but since there wasn't enough time to make sure it was perfect, it would have to do. Because he procrastinated, he had to pay over $20 to ship it overnight. Tim was upset with himself for waiting so long… again, and felt horribly ashamed when his wife exploded over the shipping cost.

All of us are guilty of second guessing ourselves, yet not all of us stop from taking action. Once you realize that you keep predicting the future as if it were 100% guaranteed to happen, you can begin to use EFT to check it out. As Tim tapped for a minute or two, an idea emerged that resolved his dilemma. He decided to give gifts of money or gift cards to specialty stores his friends or family liked. That way, the recipient could get something that was "perfect" for them.

The Eleventh Commandment

Beware of *The Eleventh Commandment* that says, "Thus it will be unto eternity." Listen to yourself and notice whether you fill your conversations with the words *always* and *never.* If so, you are creating impossible situations that can lead to procrastination. *Always* and *never,* imply that it will be this way forever. There is a sense of the eternal. You can't change it, no matter what. Dr. Burns refers to this as overgeneralization.

I am guilty of this myself. For years, I avoided driving south from my hometown on Sundays since traffic is often very heavy starting a little after noon. My husband was annoyed with me since I frequently put off going out of town with him on

Sundays for that reason. One Sunday when my husband asked me to go to shopping in the next town south I got upset. "It's *always* bumper-to-bumper. I don't want to buck the traffic," I said. "No it's not. It is only crowded occasionally," my husband argued. Finally, I made a deal with him. "If by the time we get to the Summerland exit, traffic is stopped, you have to turn around and take me home," I demanded. Of course, I was sure that I was right, and I'd prove it to him.

That evening as we were zooming home after having a great time, it dawned on me that I had not been aware of any heavy traffic going south. In fact, I hadn't even been aware of my fear until we were headed north on our way home. Now, when the opportunity to leave town on Sundays comes up I remind myself that traffic builds up frequently, but it doesn't *always* clog the freeway. Sometimes I stay in town and sometimes I leave. I am no longer imprisoned by my false fear.

When you catch yourself saying *always* and *never*, tap on your thought. I could have tapped, "Even though I am positive that traffic will be so bad on Sunday that it will take hours to go a few miles and I will be angry for wasting my time, I am giving myself a treatment now," or "Even though it is always jammed on Sunday so why am I even considering going anywhere, I am doing the best I can." The reminder phrase would be "Sunday traffic jam," "Always crowded," or "Never go south."

Like me, once you turn *always* and *never* into *frequently* and *seldom* or *occasionally*, you will definitely feel freer. Here are some examples:

♦ Even though I'll never finish sending out invitations to my party in time, I am examining this thought now. Use the reminder phrase "Never finish."

54

--

- Even though I hate that I always forget people's names, I am tapping on that now. Use the reminder phrase "Always forget."

- Even though he always criticizes me when I make a mistake, I am doing the best I can. Use the reminder phrase "He always criticizes."

- Even though I'll never get over this problem, I am open to proving myself wrong. Use the reminder phrase "Never get over it."

The Tyranny of the Should

One of the most common undermining language patterns instilled in us by our culture is the use of the word *should*. The words *should, must, ought to,* and *have to* are interpreted by procrastinators to mean, "I don't want to and you are making me!" When we say or think these words it sets up resistance and we want to drag our feet. It also makes us feel guilty if we don't follow that decree.

I *should* get my car washed. I *should* pay my bills. I *should* call my grandmother. Our lives are filled with *shoulds*. *Shoulds* keep us on the straight and narrow path to goodness. What are *shoulds* and where did they come from? Of course, we can trace them back to the original holy set, the Ten Commandments, but I am guessing that *shoulds* arose long before that.

A *should* is created when a group of people agree about how the world is or might be. This may differ from culture to culture and century to century. Democrats have different *shoulds* about the world than Republicans. Believers and non-believers differ about the *shoulds* that label us good or bad, godly or sinful. The *shoulds* of your family and friends may be diametrically opposed to those of your neighbor.

Closet Revelation

Rita said, "My closet is a mess. I should organize it. I have too many clothes that I'm not even wearing anymore. There's no more room for anything new, and I keep putting off cleaning it out. I am so disgusted with myself for being lazy." I suggested that she start tapping, and here is what she said, "Even though I am resisting organizing my closet when I really want to do it, I am exploring that now. " After each round she reported what came to mind.

♦ I am resisting.

♦ I feel annoyed with my husband because he always goes through the bag with the things I am going to give away.

♦ Feeling annoyed toward him, very annoyed.

♦ Why is he prying?

♦ I feel violated when he does this.

♦ She continued to tap five more rounds focusing on the feeling of being violated.

♦ There was no privacy in my family when I was growing up.

♦ My mother and sister read my diary when I was 10 and made fun of me

Rita kept tapping for a few more minutes on that memory when her privacy was invaded until all her anger and embarrassment were neutralized. Next, I asked her to test the effectiveness of EFT by remembering what happened and trying to feel angry and upset. She rated her emotions as zero, neutral. The following weekend she cleaned out her closet without any problem.

The famous psychiatrist Dr. Karen Horney coined the phrase "the tyranny of the should" to describe what happens when we vacillate between our "ideal self" that strives to achieve the *shoulds* and be perfect and our "despised self" that feels insecure and imperfect. Thus, *shoulds* lead to procrastination! Putting things off is often the result of your conflict with a *should*. That is because *shoulds* are inflicted on us from the outside. From our earliest years we are told what a good boy or girl *should* or *should not* do to gain approval from parent, teacher, family, community, and world. We are not given the opportunity to challenge these instructions. When we do, we may end up going our own way and marching to our own drummer, but we may also be punished and carry a load of guilt or shame about breaking away from what is expected.

Who says I should wash my car, pay my bills, and call grandma? You may say so, but where did the original rule come from and who laid it on you? Think about some of the things you are procrastinating doing right now. Pick one. Say it aloud as if someone was saying it to you with a stern voice. "Joe, you ought to do your laundry!" Whose voice did you just hear? Do you remember what was happening when you heard that voice and how you felt when you were gifted with that *should*? Take a moment to acknowledge all the guilt or shame you have felt throughout your life each time you resisted. How often have you struggled with this and other *shoulds* handed down from generation to generation?

The Cosmic ATM Technique

One way to locate the origin of the *should* is to ask the part of you that is a repository of your life experiences, your unconscious mind, for help. When you use an ordinary ATM machine, you first indicate what your business is, to deposit or withdraw money. In this case, you want to make a withdrawal. You are not going to withdraw money. You are going to extract information. When you use the ATM at a bank or store you put in your request and then wait patiently for a few seconds while the machine works to get you what you want. Finally, you get what you requested.

Pretend that you are standing in front of an ATM machine.

◆ Ask this question: How young was I when I decided that _____ was true? (Fill in with the *should* statement you chose)

◆ Take a deep breath and let it out, waiting patiently for the answer. Don't try to think of the answer.

◆ You will receive an answer in seconds. Remember that it may come as instant knowing, words in your head, a physical sensation or a picture.

Once the answer pops into your head you may remember not only how young you were, but also where you were and what was happening. If you do not remember, then do the three-step process again asking the following questions, one at a time.

◆ What was happening at the time I made the decision that this belief was the truth?

◆ Who taught me to believe this?

Sometimes just knowing the circumstances that led to your decision will be enough for you to let it go and replace it with a new truth. If not, use EFT, focusing on either the *should* or the incident surrounding it, to allow all the thoughts, feelings and memories that are associated with it to surface and be released. Then you can re-evaluate whether you want to continue to live with these *shoulds*.

Please don't think I am telling you to drop all *shoulds* and rebel against everyone and everything. That decision would result in chaos and harm. Children need *shoulds* to help them conform to the ethics of their culture and to keep them safe. However, once we are grownups we can assess those rules and decide which ones fit our beliefs and which don't.

Adults can choose which expectations they *want to* or *choose to* follow. Try this. Go back to the *should* you chose above. For instance, repeat, "I *should* do my laundry." How do you feel? Is there tension in your stomach or throat? Do you feel ashamed of yourself for being lazy? Do you want to do your laundry? If you don't, then are you willing to take the consequences? After all you are an adult and responsible for your actions. Make a decision and say either "I choose to do my laundry," or "I choose to not do my laundry." Does that feel different when you say it out loud? Most people find that when they trade in their *shoulds* for *choose to* or *choose not to*, they get rid of a load of guilt and shame. Eliminate the words *should, shouldn't, must, ought* and *have to* from your life this week and see what happens.

These common expressions indicate that the procrastinator has been putting something off and feels guilty. Add yours to the list.

♦ I should vacuum the carpet/clean the bathroom/fold my laundry.

♦ I shouldn't eat too much at Christmas.

♦ I have to pay my bills.

♦ I must remember to visit my grandparents this weekend.

♦ I ought to start going to the gym regularly.

There is another category of *shoulds* that I call the *hidden shoulds* since they are implied but not stated. Once you become attuned to listening for *shoulds*, you will also find yourself pinpointing those that are not said audibly. For instance,

♦ "I slept too late again and missed going to the gym" implies that you *should* go to the gym.

♦ "I ate too much at the buffet," means that you *should* eat less.

♦ "I hate myself when I get a late charge on my credit card" means that you *should* pay on time.

Keep telling yourself that grown-ups don't need *shoulds*. Adults have the right to do whatever they want (as long as it isn't illegal or harmful to others) if they are willing to accept the consequences. We can trade in our *shoulds* for choose to or choose not to. Start to listen to yourself and decide what you really want to do. If you can't decide then tap on the thought using the Be Your Own Best Friend variation and see what happens.

Write to Dear Abby

An interesting exercise to practice picking out *Stinkin' Thinkin'* is to write a paragraph as if you were writing to Dear Abby or a favorite wise advisor, in which you pour out your despair over your procrastination problem. Tell Abby what specifically you are procrastinating about and why. Maybe you need to clean out your closet or garage, be on time for an important occasion, get started on your holiday shopping, write thank you notes after your wedding, etc. Follow these steps.

♦ Write a long paragraph to Dear Abby.

♦ Re-read what you just wrote and see if you are practicing some kind of *Stinkin' Thinkin'* (All or Nothing, Crystal Ball Gazing, Eleventh Commandment, Shoulds). Circle the phrases or sentences and name the kind of *Stinkin' Thinkin'* you are engaging in.

♦ Use EFT on each of those beliefs and see if you are able to change your thoughts or feelings.

Theresa's letter might read like this:

Dear Abby,

I am a fifty-year-old divorcee who needs a job. I haven't had to work in thirty years, and I am very nervous about finding employment. Although I have taken a brush-up class in typing and using computers, I don't have faith in myself. I start out every day telling myself I should look for work, but watch TV for hours, talk on the phone with friends, and do everything but read the want ads or go on interviews. Sometimes I don't even get dressed. When they see how overweight I am no one will want me. I don't know how to motivate myself. Please help.

Thanks for your advice,
Theresa

Can you find the *Stinkin' Thinkin'* in this note? There are a few *shoulds*; one is obvious and the others are hidden. She says, "I *should* look for work." The hidden *shoulds* that are not stated are, she *should* read the want ads and go for interviews, and she *should* lose weight. Theresa is also doing Crystal Ball Gazing. She knows for certain that they won't hire her. We might say that she is including the Eleventh Commandment as well when she says *no one will want me,* because it sounds like she means no one will *ever* want me, so why bother to leave the house.

After Theresa confronted her *Stinkin' Thinkin'*, she felt
more confident about herself. Within a short time, a friend
recommended her to someone who offered her a fascinating job
that she excelled at and loved doing. She didn't have to answer
any ads or go through rigorous interviews after all.

When you decide to pay attention to your thoughts and to what
comes out of your mouth, you will be flabbergasted at how you
create a reality that is neither reasonable nor kind. Now that you
know what to look for, you can tap away the negative and install
a positive outlook on life. When the fears dissolve, so do the
obstacles to moving forward.

Chapter 6

Biological Roots:
Your Brain Is to Blame

You may be having a hard time today. Perhaps you feel
depressed because you're behind on important projects
and hate yourself because you're not living up to your best
intentions. Cheer up. There are three things that I want you to
know. One: you aren't lazy, stupid or weak. Two: at the core of
procrastination is fear. Three: it all starts in the brain. Does that
mean that you're not to blame? Maybe.

Dr. Clinton Kilts, Vice Chairman of Research and Professor at
Emory College, believes, "There is nothing that you do, there is
no thought that you have, there is no awareness, there is no lack
of awareness, there is nothing that mars your daily existence
that doesn't have a neural code." As you learn more about how
your wonderful brain works you can understand how your
behaviors came into being.

Get to Know Your Brain

The well-known healer Carolyn Myss said that our biology
is our biography. Science is constantly finding out new ways
to explain how what we do and how we feel originate in our

amazing brain. Neuroscientists tell us that we are conscious
of only five percent of our thinking. That means ninety-five
percent lies at the level beyond awareness. We are not conscious
of most of our decisions, actions, emotions and behavior.

There are three parts of your brain that you need to know
about in order to understand and overcome procrastination: the
brain stem, the prefrontal cortex and the limbic system. The
brain stem is the lower part of your brain. It is close to and is
continuous with your spinal cord. The brain stem is in charge
of the functions we need in order to stay alive: breathing,
digestion, and blood circulation.

The prefrontal cortex is an area of the brain behind your
forehead. This part of the brain is your executive branch. It
orchestrates thoughts and actions in accordance with your
internal goals. The prefrontal cortex determines good and bad
and can predict outcomes as well as suppress urges.

The limbic system is attached to the prefrontal cortex and is
sometimes called the reptilian part of the brain. The limbic
system is unique and very important in understanding what
makes you tick. It is thought to be the part of the body that
maintains and guides the emotions and behaviors necessary for
self-preservation and survival of the species. It is involved with
emotions, motivation and memory. The limbic system doesn't
think in words; it just feels emotions. There is no time in the
limbic system. The past and the present exist simultaneously!
Keep these facts in mind since they will help you have
appreciation for your perplexing behavior as we go along.

Within the limbic system are two structures you may have
heard about, the hippocampus and the amygdala. The
hippocampus, the main memory-processing center, is the

repository of your memories from the time you were about two onward. The amygdala, the region of the brain responsible for processing emotional memories, is like a smoke alarm. It works around the clock sensing danger in your environment. Studies of fear conditioning conclude that the amygdala plays a major role in linking external stimuli to defense responses. That means that if there is danger, the amygdala signals the rest of the brain, which immediately creates a survival reaction. The amygdala may send a Yellow Alert to the thinking brain when the risk seems mild. However, if the danger seems extremely threatening, it signals a Red Alert that sends the body into an immediate survival reaction of Fight, Flight, or Freeze.

Through the years since your birth, you've had many happy times, but along the way, you've also had moments that were stressful, fearful and downright dangerous. When something very unpleasant happened to you, the amygdala went into Red Alert and your body responded to protect you. All of this happened in the blink of an eye. There was no time to think about it, so the prefrontal cortex, the thinking part of the brain, was bypassed. However, that moment was stored as a panoramic memory that might include what was happening, details of the surroundings, sounds and even smells that were present. When the danger subsided, the thinking brain came back online again. This mechanism for storing memories of physically or emotionally threatening moments developed when humankind first evolved in order to protect our survival.

At different times, every one of us has experienced what it is like when this mechanism is triggered because evolution has created these responses to promote survival when we face present and future threats. A part of the brain called the thalamus tells the amygdala what is happening right now. Another part, the hypothalamus conveys what the outcome was the last time it happened. Then the amygdala makes a decision. This happens so rapidly we are not aware of these steps. We just react. We are at the mercy of our helping brain. This reaction is hardwired in the brain. The only problem is that the hair trigger amygdala sometimes over-reacts to supposed dangers that no longer exist.

Scientists have discovered that the brain has an inherent need to make sense of what we experience. Therefore, we rationalize after the fact to explain to ourselves, "What the heck was that all about?" After a frightening episode, some people decide, "I must have deserved that because I am bad," while others resolve, "I survived. I am a lucky person." Some think, "I deserve to be criticized or laughed at so I'd better not put myself in a position where that might happen again." These decisions made along life's journey stay with you and mold your adult behavior. They often lead to actions of putting things off, not even beginning them, or failing to complete them, that will assist you to avoid experiencing that again.

We know now that the amygdala and the hippocampus set each other off during the recall of highly emotional memories. Apparently, emotion can trigger recollection, and vice versa. The emotion enhances recollection, but at the same time, by bringing certain events to mind, you also relive the emotional response. It is this kind of memory loop that underlies procrastination.

They Were Stopped Cold

Margaret was a thirty-year-old single woman who kept putting off moving out of her mother's house into her own apartment. When she was very little Margaret often saw her father beat her mother. She would hide under the table and try to be invisible. The tiny girl decided that she had to avoid her raging parent and keep away from being noticed or she would be hurt too. She decided that all angry people are dangerous. Her brain recorded both the facial expressions of anger and the words and tone of anger.

Allthough her parents had been divorced for many years, and her mother had taken charge of her own life, Margaret was afraid to tell her mother she wanted to leave because she might make her mother angry, and angry people can get violent. Margaret would do anything to avoid someone else's wrath, even stop herself from becoming independent.

Every time Margaret imagined making her mother mad, her amygdala ingeniously matched the present stressful situation with her scary memories of her raging father. Since there is no differentiation between the past and the present in the limbic system, just thinking about mother's possible displeasure caused Margaret to relive the terror from the past as if it were still occurring, substituting her mother as an angry person instead of her father.

Even if there is only a ten percent match, it is enough for the guardian amygdala to signal the Red Alert. Instead of thinking about the present situation, she reacted the same way she did all those years ago. She shut her mouth and ran away from the possibility of incurring a look of annoyance on mother's face.

Another person who was still living out the decision she made as a child was Lily. Lily was working at a very boring, low paying job despite her education and ability. She kept finding excuses for not going back to school to prepare for a career.

It turned out that, as a child, she had been traumatized when her teacher embarrassed her in front of the entire kindergarten class. Lily froze. She couldn't say anything because she was so mortified. As a result, she decided that the teacher was right and she was stupid. She vowed that she would never let herself be caught in front of a group where she could be embarrassed.

Lily procrastinated about pursuing more schooling. She turned into a five-year-old at the thought of what might happen if she went back to a classroom again. She felt safe in her present job even if it was a dead end.

Like many other procrastinators, Lily and Margaret sought help by reading books and went for counseling. One of the most popular modalities recommended to treat procrastination is Cognitive Therapy, where the emphasis is on pinpointing self-defeating thoughts and beliefs and changing them. The idea is that pessimistic thinking leads to negative emotions that lead to procrastination.

However, recent studies have shown that emotions come before thoughts. Dr. Daniel J. Siegel, well-known researcher and author, claims that emotions exist at a stage before we have language and drive the brain towards deciding on an appropriate reaction to a particular situation. Only then do the thoughts start.

That is why changing negative thoughts will not always help you stop procrastinating. The intense urge to keep yourself from getting hurt again has no words. You may find yourself procrastinating, and if pressed you may have an emotional response like, "I am afraid it won't be good enough." or, "If I do it well, they'll expect me to keep doing it perfectly all the time." In order to transform your negative thoughts, you need to go back to the time of the initial emotional reaction... the time when you first created that belief as the truth for you. To do this, you need the help of your amygdala and your hippocampus.

Two Kinds of Memory

There are two kinds of memories stored in our body, explicit memories and implicit memories. Explicit memories are autobiographical. You can remember yourself being there. They are like movies in your head or pictures in a photo album. We all can remember both happy and unhappy events we participated in like birthday parties, going to the circus or falling off our bike. Margaret and Lily's behavior resulted from terrible events they remembered clearly.

However, scientists believe that ninety-five percent of brain activity takes place beyond our conscious awareness. Most of our everyday decisions and information is stored as implicit memories. It is astounding to realize how much of what we do is determined by mysterious memories and the emotional forces associated with those memories.

Implicit memories are recollections of what our body experiences during trauma. They are hardwired in the brain. These memories are acquired in a flash and stored for our lifetime unless we recognize and clear them. When the amygdala signals the Red Alert, these unconscious memories are unleashed instantly as a survival mechanism in the face of perceived danger. Then we re-experience the scary past as though it were happening in the present.

Implicit memories go back to birth and can influence our present behavior even if we are totally unaware of them. My friend June can't stand to wear anything around her neck. Wearing high collars, especially turtleneck tops, sends her into a state of panic. Although she didn't get upset when she thought about necklaces or tight collars, she reacted when her body felt them. She couldn't figure out where this strange fear came from until she discovered that she had been born with the umbilical cord wound tightly around her neck and she almost choked to

69

--

death at birth. Although her conscious mind did not remember that, her body did.

There are times when we can't account for our actions by thinking back to something that happened to us, no matter how hard we try because that information is unavailable to our conscious mind.

A Dark and Scary Tale

This was the case with Rebecca, who was afraid to fly and avoided anything that would necessitate a plane trip. Unfortunately, she couldn't get out of an important business trip to another country. She came to me because she needed to overcome her fear of flying. She wasn't as afraid of being in the air as she was of being in an enclosed space. Rebecca was able to understand that her procrastination was a direct result of a fear of being in closed spaces, but how did that fear originate?

As Rebecca and I explored her past she was able to remember other times when she panicked in a closed space, like the time when she went camping and had to sleep in the tiny compartment behind the truck's cab, or the time she went to an underground cavern and had to be carried out due to her panic. Rebecca didn't remember the first time it happened, although my intuition told me that it started much earlier in her life. She described the sensation as being in a dark place where the air wasn't moving.

When I asked Rebecca's unconscious mind how young she could be the first time she was in a dark place where the air wasn't moving, she began to hyperventilate and had trouble breathing. She suddenly said, "You know I was a breech birth." Her body remembered the birth struggle even though her conscious mind didn't. Every time Rebecca had been or might be in a small, dark, or enclosed space where the air was limited, her body relived the original moments of birth and she experienced inexplicable feelings of terror. Since there is no time in the limbic system, the past is always present.

An implicit memory involves an automatic reaction without any recollection. To stop her body from reliving the terror of that moment, Rebecca used EFT saying, "Even though something traumatic happened to me at birth that is still affecting me, I am ready to free myself of this problem." After two EFT sessions, she got on the plane and had a successful trip. When she returned she called me to say that she felt like a new person.

Retrain Your Brain

Memories of awful happenings are very hard to extinguish. We have to retrain our brains. EFT can actually disconnect the fear loop that was put in place a long time ago. According to Dr. Ronald Rudin, clinician and scientist, EFT raises the serotonin level in the brain. Serotonin is a brain chemical that plays an important role in mood regulation, allowing a person to feel calm. In addition to raising serotonin, EFT also helps raise the levels of two other brain substances, glutamate and GABA, which are also involved in de-linking the loop.

Dr. Rudin suggests that you picture the amygdala like a beach filled with holes. Each hole represents a painful emotion, event or memory. When you focus on that unpleasant memory or emotion and stimulate EFT energy points, that hole in the beach fills with glutamate. Then when a serotonin wave flows in, the chemical GABA is released, allowing that particular glutamate-filled hole to interact with the serotonin and solidify. The hole is now gone. The negative reaction cannot take place anymore.

71

--

Although you may still remember what happened to you, you will no longer feel any intense emotion. It will be as if you are looking at a photo in an album, just another memory. If, like Rebecca, only your body remembers the original memory, it will stop reacting to the old trigger.

After using EFT, Margaret finally told her mother that she wanted to move out, and nothing horrible happened to her. Lily realized that the past was past and the mean teacher could no longer harm her. She could go to school and prepare for a better future or seek a better job.

Each time you treat your brain and release the fear response with EFT, the prefrontal cortex (your thinking brain) can re-evaluate your earlier decision and replace it with a new and healthier one. Unfettered by the past, you can easily move forward without being hindered by the ghosts of what went before.

Chapter 7

What's Holding You Back
From Moving Forward?

What do these people all have in common? Zach missed the deadline for handing in a quarterly report at work and was reprimanded by his boss. Kathy filled her garage with so many boxes that she couldn't park her car in it. Anthony kept postponing taking the test to get into graduate school, and Beverly delayed finding an office for her new business. What do these four people have in common? "That's easy," you may think. They are all playing the waiting game.

Why are they willing to put up with the dire consequences of dragging their feet? Zach is passed over for a promotion, Kathy's boyfriend is on the verge of breaking up with her because she's so messy, Anthony is anxious and depressed, and Beverly can't get her business going. No, they aren't lazy, stupid or weak. Their lack of initiative results from False Beliefs. What kind of thoughts could be so intense that a person would rather hold back from completing a project and be willing to suffer the negative outcome rather than go ahead with a goal that seems simple or desirable?

The Five False Beliefs that keep most procrastinators from moving forward are:

♦ Failure is unacceptable.

♦ People will dislike, ridicule, exclude or harm me if I don't do it right.

♦ Success is dangerous.

♦ I'm afraid of what the future holds.

♦ I don't wanna and you can't make me!

Experiences you had earlier in your life led you to make decisions that have remained in your unconscious mind ever since. These False Beliefs have been the stage directions in your life story up to now. You are so used to feeling the anxiety generated by the False Beliefs that you may not even be aware of them. Eventually the fears are covered over with your excuses so you are no longer in touch with them.

Worst Case Scenario

One way to rid yourself of the consequences of your False Beliefs is to play the *Worst Case Scenario Game.* Ask yourself, "What is the worst thing that will happen if I clean out my garage, pay my taxes, go for my mammogram, send Christmas cards in time for the holiday, sign up for school, wash my car etc?" Write or say aloud the first thing that comes to mind. Don't judge yourself on your answer.

Ask again, making sure you use the phrase, *I'm afraid,* because that is what this is all about. Keep this up until you have run out of the easy answers like, "I'll be happy" or "I'll be healthy." Eventually you'll hit pay dirt. The answer that springs to mind may have nothing to do with the project you are dawdling over. That is the point. Once you find out which False Belief is to blame, use EFT to reassess it and install a new and reasonable alternative.

Zach's False Beliefs

When Zach tried this method, he discovered two False Beliefs: *failure is unacceptable* and *people will dislike, ridicule, exclude or harm me if I don't do it right*. He was afraid that although he might think his report was good, his boss might have different standards that were higher. His worst fear was that he would be a laughing stock if his report weren't perfect. He always had to be perfect. He used EFT, saying, "I am now releasing all the times and all the ways I have harmed myself because I believed that failure was unacceptable." He decided to ask a trusted friend to look over his work in the future and give him feedback when he doubted himself.

The Secrets In Her Garage

Kathy found out that she was one of many whose behavior symbolizes *I don't wanna, and you can't make me!* She just didn't want to do the boring chore of organizing and cleaning her garage. She started to tap on those words and said, "Even though the garage is a mess and I should clean it up, I don't want to and I am willing to explore why."

Tapping revealed that when she was a teenager her authoritarian father would never let her meet her friends at the mall on Saturday until she had completed all the chores he set out for her. He was mean, and she was still sticking her tongue out at him.

The more her boyfriend nagged her, the more he reminded her of her father. No one was going to boss her around like her dad! She felt the anger in her solar plexus and continued to tap. Finally, she knew that she was no longer under her father's thumb and she could clean up her garage because it would please herself, not because she had to.

As she tapped, Kathy also realized that she was procrastinating because of a *fear of what the future holds*. If she cleaned out her garage, she would have to give away the toys her daughter had outgrown. That reminded her that her daughter was growing up and would soon graduate from school and leave home. Not cleaning the garage meant not having to look at the toys and face her sadness about what was to come.

Love, Marriage and Grad School

Anthony also feared what the future might hold. When he thought about the worst-case scenario he imagined himself in graduate school meeting new people. He would become friendly with intelligent people who were interested in what he was studying. A thought popped into his head. What if he met a woman who was more interesting than his wife! He might find his wife boring. Would graduate school ruin his marriage? A few rounds of EFT allowed him to feel reassured that he could go to school and stay married.

Finding a Mate

Beverly figured out that her fear of being a success in business stemmed from the False Belief, *success is dangerous*. When she pondered the *Worst Case Scenario* if she opened her own office, she immediately said, "If I am too successful, no man will want to marry me and take care of me."

As she tapped, she told me that each time she went office hunting and imagined her name on the door, she heard her mother's voice inside her head whispering, "If you are too independent what man will want to marry you and take care of you?" Her mother's generation was mostly homemakers who thought their mission in life was to look good and make a lovely home for their husbands. What if her mother was right? Would she jeopardize her chances if she competed successfully with men?

After using EFT, she knew without a doubt that she could be as successful as she wanted to be. As she continued to tap and focus on this thought, she remembered reading a quote by Gloria Steinem who said, "Some of us are becoming the men we wanted to marry." She soon found the "perfect" office and then found the "perfect" man.

Too Many Books

Another person whose False Belief caused great misery was Clara, who had moved from a large home to a small apartment after her divorce. She was a book lover and kept procrastinating about going through the 3,000 books she had taken with her. There was no room in her new home for so many books and she couldn't part with any of them. When I asked Clara about the worst thing that would happen if she parted with some of these books, she finally blurted out, "What if the answer to the secret of life is in one of these books, and I give it away?" As she used EFT to explore this irrational fear, she realized that most likely all the books she owned were available in a library, a bookstore, or online if she needed to replace them.

Logrolling

Disorganized desks, closets, garages, and file cabinets are often not what they seem. Procrastinators fixate on cleaning or clearing out some space, starting or ending a new project, but that may not be the primary problem. It is often the symbol of another deeper issue.

When procrastinators link together two problems that are completely dissimilar, they often become paralyzed and unable to solve either one. I call this thinking process *logrolling*. Logrolling

Is a term used in politics to describe how politicians trade votes for their mutual benefit. For instance, if the senator from one state needs support for her bill about improving transportation, she may contact the senator from another state who proposes a bill about farming. They create legislation that includes both transportation and farming aid and push it through, although these two areas have nothing to do with each other.

Doris was so fed up with her messy desk that she finally sought help by attending one of my workshops. No matter how many times she promised herself that she would clean it up, she put many other things first. "It's not a big desk. I should be able to finish the job in a few hours," she said. I proceeded to play the *Worst Case Scenario Game* with Doris in order to find her underlying False Belief.

"What is the worst thing that will happen if you clean up your desk?" I asked. "I'll feel better," she replied. "Then what are you afraid will happen?" "It will look better." "And then what?" "I'll have time to clean out the bookcase." I pushed and pushed, asking her to imagine the very worst after each of her comebacks, until the light dawned. "If I clean up my desk I'll have to clean up my life, and I'll have to divorce my husband," she blurted out. No wonder she wasn't able to get her desk in order. She was putting off exploring an issue that her conscious mind was unwilling to contemplate. Although I did not know whether Doris's marriage was in trouble or whether this was just a fantasy, the thought startled and upset her.

Doris' dilemma was a perfect example of *logrolling*. What does a messy desk have to do with marriage? Nothing, except in this case the desk seemed to be a metaphor for something "messy" in her life. One of the reasons I don't discuss time management techniques or how to organize your belongings in this book is for exactly this reason. Doris's problem was not her desk. It was her marriage. Using the *Worst Case Scenario* approach helped Doris freed herself to organize her desk.

I suggested that she use EFT to address her feelings about her marriage using one or more of these focusing statements:

♦ "Even though a part of me is unwilling to look at the state of my marriage, I am exploring that now."

♦ "Even though, I am not happy with my marriage and am avoiding looking into that by distracting myself with my messy desk, I am doing the best I can.

♦ " Even though I know there are problems in my marriage, I am willing to tap about them now."

How To Stay Single

Another person whose procrastination was based on *logrolling* was Ed. Ed, a divorced man, was a do-it-yourselfer who remodeled his kitchen and bathroom, but six months later still hadn't put the knobs on the kitchen cabinets. He was exasperated and angry with himself for shirking the job. After he finished his tale of woe, I insisted on asking him the *Worst Case Scenario* questions. After a few rounds, there was a long pause. Finally, Ed said, "If I complete my house I won't have any more excuses to not invite people over and socialize." "And then what is the worst thing that could happen?" I asked. "I'll have to get married again!"

Once Ed heard himself state his fear, he instantly understood that fixing his house had nothing to do with marriage, except symbolically. He didn't have to invite people over whether his house was perfect or not, and he certainly didn't need to get married again unless and until he chose to.

Desks and kitchens don't have anything to do with marriage. It's all just *logrolling*. Now that you know how this irrational thinking works, you can look out for *logrolling* and use the *Worst Case Scenario* game and EFT to challenge your thinking.

The Weighting Game

"I'll start on Monday" is the universal dieter's excuse. I call this waiting game a *weighting game*. Putting off taking it off is a common behavior, even when people who want to lose weight are motivated by a strong desire to be healthier and look good.

Dieters suffer from the same False Beliefs that I have already discussed. Fear of falling off the diet or not reaching goal weight, fear of what others will think of how you look, fear of success once you look great, and fear of failing by gaining it back in the future may be at work. Looking for the unstated False Beliefs, playing the *Worst Case Scenario* and using EFT helped these women turn things around.

The columnist, Art Buchwald, once said that the word *diet* comes from the verb *to die* because that is how you feel when you are on a diet. Although he was joking, the fear of death is sometimes behind delaying weight loss. One of the students in my class for overeaters was Alice who was almost six feet tall and weighed 270 pounds. Unbeknownst to me, she had been molested by her father. Alice prided herself on her strength and boasted that not even her husband could overpower her. During the first week of her diet, she raced to the emergency room thinking she was having a heart attack. Fortunately, it was only a panic attack, but she stopped her diet and couldn't seem to get back on track. Her hidden fear turned out to be that if she lost weight someone could hurt or overwhelm her.

Because Alice had been abused when she was younger and had not healed from her childhood trauma, it was important for her to work with a therapist to deal with these underlying issues before she could allow herself to lose weight. EFT is an excellent technique for healing the wounds of abuse without re-traumatizing a person, but this kind of work should only be done with a licensed professional.

Vivian and Olivia also feared death. Vivian was afraid that if she lost weight it would mean she had cancer, since many people with cancer lose a lot of weight. Olivia's family was killed in the holocaust, and she was afraid that if another holocaust occurred and she was too thin, she would starve to death in a concentration camp. These types of fears are hidden in the unconscious, so people are usually very surprised when they surface. Using a focusing statement like, "Even though I am terrified that if I lose weight it means I have cancer, I am tapping on that now," or "Even though I am scared to be thin since I might be vulnerable if I am deprived or mistreated, I want to let go of that fear now," helped these women eliminate their irrational *fears of success.*

Another example of *fear of success* and *fear of the future* has to do with success and sex. Although Carol was happily married, she was afraid that if she lost weight she wouldn't be able to control her sexual appetite and would be unfaithful. Rose was also married and feared that, although she loved her husband of twenty-five years, she would be attracted to other women and want to have lesbian relationships. Both these women kept unconsciously sabotaging their efforts to reach their weight loss goals until they brought their fears to light and tapped about them. Rose knew that she had never had sexual desires for women, so why should she start now? She also acknowledged how much she loved and desired her husband. Carol also realized that she was happy and satisfied with her husband, and liked being monogamous.

Eileen and Samantha were worried about what their families would think if they were svelte. They might be disliked, ridiculed or excluded. Eileen was terrified that if she became thin she would be prettier than her sister Beth. Everyone in the family acknowledged that Beth was a babe while Eileen was the brainy one. If she stepped out of her role in the family, she unconsciously feared that they would stop loving her.

81
--

Every time Samantha visited home, her petite mother would drag her into the bathroom and weigh her to make sure that Samantha didn't weigh less than mom did. Fears of disapproval kept them fat.

Obviously Eileen could benefit from using EFT to explore the messages she received as she was growing up that led to her decision that she should know her place in the family and stay there. Samantha also needed to find out why and when she decided that she wasn't allowed to go against the destructive wishes of an unloving mother. I will discuss these issues in Chapter 9, Digging Up the Roots of Procrastination.

Tapping on these problems might sound like this:

♦ Even though I am not supposed to outdo my mother/sister or they won't love me anymore, I completely love and accept myself.

♦ Even though I am always trying to live up to my family's expectations, but it means I can't be true to myself, and then I overeat, I deserve to feel better.

♦ Even though I am an adult now, and don't have to listen to or obey their demands or fulfill their needs, I am scared to stop, and I am treating this fear now.

Krista's husband frequently nagged her to lose weight. He didn't want to make love with her because she was overweight. She felt unlovable and wanted to please him. She said she would sign up for Weight Watchers but didn't follow through. At times, she would be "good," then go on horrendous binges and regain all that she lost. She couldn't seem to reach her goal. When she came face to face with her worst-case *fear of the future* it was that if she got thin she would discover that her husband still didn't find her attractive! Tapping helped her decide to ask her husband to go for some couples counseling to work on this problem.

President Franklin D. Roosevelt said, "The only thing we have to fear is fear itself." That is what the "weighting game" is about. All the excuses dieters use really hide an unconscious fear that something awful will happen if they succeed. Yet, usually when the fear is brought to light, it can be confronted and eliminated.

You now have a clear picture of how False Beliefs can run your life, distort your thoughts and cause you to procrastinate. I hope that you have recognized yourself in the examples I have shared. Use the tools you have learned to attack the negative beliefs and free yourself. Soon you will be able to laugh at how you used to think.

Chapter 8

Perfect or Else

Not all perfectionists are procrastinators, but many procrastinators find that their lives are made more difficult because of their worry about things being perfect. The trouble with perfectionism is that there are no concrete guidelines against which to measure bona fide perfectionism. Each purist stakes out an area in his life in which his need for perfection becomes overwhelming, while in other sectors of his life things are "good enough." Some perfectionists are detail oriented while others are uncompromising about rules and structure. Another group's behavior is influenced by their need to avoid mistakes. Most perfectionists worry about how they will look to others. They are likely to procrastinate to avoid judgment.

A client brought this to my attention recently. Jayne was complaining about her husband who, in her opinion, was both a perfectionist and a chronic procrastinator. Since she suffered from back problems it was difficult for her to make the bed, and her helpful husband had assumed that chore. According to Jayne, she had to remind the procrastinator to do this simple task almost every day, and even then, all he did was to throw the blankets willy-nilly over the bed and walk away. She commented, "Although he is finicky about how things look, he puts off making the bed and doesn't do a careful job. I have to do it all over again after he is through."

Apparently, that morning as she was getting dressed, she had to remind him of his promise. Then, when she noticed that he was making the bed his way, she called to him, "Jerry, don't bother. You know I am going to make the bed again the *right way*." Her spouse replied, "Of course, Madam Perfectionist." Jayne was bewildered. "How dare he call me a perfectionist? This from a man who took a year to complete making bookcases for the living room and got upset because they were 1/100 of an inch off."

Jayne continued, "Am I a perfectionist because I want to smooth the creases from the sheets, fluff the pillows and straighten the blankets so the wrinkles don't show? It's not as if I measure how many inches the comforter hangs off the floor. I don't demand hospital corners." Jayne admitted that they both found the moment funny and had a good laugh over which one was the real perfectionist, however it still bugged her.

She didn't think she was expecting too much by wanting to have her husband make the bed the *right way*, yet the definition of *right* is what started their disagreement. People who are sticklers for doing things *right* are perfectionists if their standards are irrationally high. Who decides what is too high? There's the rub. Although Jerry was a stickler for perfection in his wood working projects, he didn't seem to care if the bed was neat. After much discussion, Jerry revealed that his procrastination about making the bed and doing it carefully was really his "I don't wanna and you can't make me" reaction when his wife acted like a critical mother.

Are You a Perfectionistic Procrastinator?

Let's explore the relationship between perfectionism and procrastination by looking at the dynamics of perfectionism. People are not born with the need to be perfect. Tiny tots are like puppies and kittens. They are un-self conscious. Then something happens to change things.

The roots of perfectionism lie in those early years when the approval of parents or caretakers is vital for us to flourish. Approval means love. When parents are hard to please, the child begins to fear making mistakes and, in order to get love, develops ways to avoid failure. She decides that perfection is necessary to get her needs met, however perfection is only attainable if she does things right.

This leads to emotional stress. The child develops anxiety about any occurrence in which there is no guarantee of success. This culminates in the belief that failure is dangerous and undesirable. This set of circumstances is what creates a perfectionist.

Procrastination results because there is no guarantee that the child's effort will pay off. The perfectionist must keep avoiding the negative outcome he imagines will result if his endeavor isn't good enough, because without the needed loving approval, he believes that something awful will happen. This can lead to the creation of standards that are impossible to live up to. I have often questioned the people in my classes who are struggling with the consequences of their perfectionism, asking if they have ever met a *perfect* person. No one has come up with an example yet.

Perfectionistic procrastinators often tell themselves:

♦ I must be perfect or I will be rejected.

♦ If I make a mistake, I will be humiliated.

♦ If I don't set the highest standards for myself, I am likely to end up a second rate person.

♦ I shouldn't have to repeat the same mistake twice.

♦ If I can't do something really well, there is little point in doing it.

♦ An average performance is unacceptable to me.

♦ If I make a mistake, I am worthless.

How did you come to believe some of these self-defeating ideas? If you are ready to explore letting go of perfectionism, use the *Cosmic ATM Technique* you learned in Chapter 5. Pretend that you are standing in front of an ATM machine. Choose one or more statements from the above list that are the most true for you. Select one at a time. Imagine yourself in front of the ATM making your request.

♦ Ask this question: How young was I when I decided that _____ was true? (Fill in with the statement you chose from the previous list or make up one of your own)

♦ Take a deep breath and let it out, waiting patiently for the answer. Don't try to think of the answer.

♦ You will receive an answer. Remember that it may come as instant knowing, words in your head, or a picture.

Then do the three step process again asking the following questions, one at a time.

♦ What was happening at the time I made the decision that this belief was the truth?

♦ Who taught me to believe this?

Perhaps just knowing what happened will be enough for you to let it go and replace it with a new truth. If not, use EFT, focusing on either the negative belief about perfection or the incident surrounding it, to allow all the thoughts, feelings and memories that are associated with it to surface and be released. Then you can re-evaluate whether you want to continue to live with this conviction.

The Stress of Achieving A's

Nicole chose, *If I don't set the highest standards for myself, I am likely to end up a second rate person.* When she asked the question, she learned that she was 10 years old, and a memory popped into her head. Although she was a very good student in school, getting excellent marks most of the time, Nicole recalled a scene where her mother was reading her report card and asked, "Only a B+?" In that moment, she decided that anything less than an A was an embarrassment.

Once she understood that a decision she made when she was 10 was still ruling her life, she used EFT saying, "Even though that moment when my mother criticized my report card, and I decided that I had to get all A's, has caused me a great deal of pain, I love and accept myself. As she tapped, she was able to let go of the guilt and shame she felt at her mother's words. After a few more rounds, she felt a surge of happiness about what an intelligent and capable person she actually was and had always been, no matter what the grade was. Soon she let go of the resentment toward her mother as she acknowledged all the other ways mother had supported and encouraged Nicole over the years.

Like Mother, Like Daughter

Nancy said that she was "drowning in things to do" and didn't know where to start. Her bedroom was a mess, filled with magazines and papers she had to read to stay current in her job. Meanwhile she was spending a lot of time keeping the rest of her home looking perfect. When I suggested that her children were old enough to help with cleaning chores, she said that it wouldn't be good enough for her. That's why she had to do it herself, although it sapped her energy and kept her depressed

Nancy was trapped by the belief that *an average performance is unacceptable*. In answer to the question, "Who taught me to believe this?" she exclaimed, "I have turned into my mother!" Nancy explained that despite the fact that mom was fastidious and demanding, her own bedroom was usually dusty and less than perfect. After using EFT to examine the ways she had taken on her mother's idiosyncrasies, Nancy was soon able to delegate chores to her children and feel less stressed about having to do it all herself.

Write Your Resignation

It is easy to be angry with or hate our parents or siblings when we suffered at their hands. However, few of us are able to have compassion for those people until much later in life, if ever, or to realize that their behaviors resulted from the tragedies and wounds they suffered. Perhaps you can intellectually understand that they were usually doing their best, and their best was pretty awful, but the pain inside of you is still throbbing.

One way to break the chains that bind you to negative beliefs about being *perfect or else* is to write a letter of resignation to the ones who inflicted these beliefs upon you. Tell them that you are no longer available to live under those rules. Relate all the ways you have harmed yourself by trying to be perfect. Tell them that they can continue to believe what they want but you are now an adult and can do what you want, even if they disagree. Close by declaring what you now choose to do to live a new and different life.

If you can't think of a person to write to, address your letter directly to the negative belief itself. When you are through you can hold a short ceremony in which you read the letter aloud and proclaim yourself free. Some people like to burn it up in a fireplace or outdoor grill. Others tear it into little pieces and throw it out or bury it.

Dear "If I make a mistake I will be rejected,"
You have been discovered, and you are nothing but bullshit! You are very objectionable and have made my life miserable. I have not allowed myself to try new things because of you. I have put pressure on myself and on my children to believe in you. Now I feel guilty for what I have done to them. You have held me back and I am tired of it. You will have no more power over me as of today. You have served your purpose, but now I am kicking you out. So long! I can't say your stay has been fun. Sincerely,
Your name goes here

Punishment or Rewards

The implied promise in perfectionism is that being perfect brings rewards. I don't think any perfectionist I have met has ever felt perfect enough. It is like the greyhound that chases the decoy. You never seem to get the prize. Let's examine this phenomenon more closely.

How perfect do you have to be, and what reward will you receive if you are good enough? Are you seeking the love or approval of one special person? Ken could never live up to his father's expectations, no matter what he did. Even when he was the valedictorian of his class, his father found fault with his speech. What if that person whose stamp of approval you must have is now dead? Where does that leave you?

Is there a time limit you have set for yourself? How long do you have to push yourself to achieve perfection, and how much do you have to suffer before you can relax and be OK? In one of my workshops, I asked the class to draw a picture of their problem. One woman drew a scene of herself on a treadmill. Above her head was a cartoon balloon filled with curse words. I think that depicts how most perfectionists experience life. They live as if they are on a perpetual journey that has no end. They just keep miserably plugging along.

Let's suppose that you actually reach your goal. You are deemed perfect or good enough by those whose words you have been waiting for all these years. How will your life be different? Will anything change? I once met a man who had won a prestigious award for writing a best-selling book. He made a lot of money. Then he experienced writer's block and stopped writing. He couldn't create a new work because he told himself that he had to write another prizewinner. Since there was no guarantee that it would be a best seller, he couldn't risk failure.

If you aren't perfect, what bad thing will happen to you? I can't think of any worse thing than the misery you are already living. The inspiring teacher and author, Ken Keyes said, "To be upset over what I don't have is to waste what I do have." Each day that you judge yourself less than, a failure, unlovable, unworthy, etc, is a day lost forever. Perfectionists are always living in the future and don't get to enjoy the now.

Dare Yourself to Fail

Like Nicole, my need to excel and get A's kept me from trying out new things early in my life. One of the activities I shied away from was doing crafts or learning sports that I knew I would do poorly. One of the things I always wanted to do was learn to make things with clay, but since I was worried about what people would think I would never try. Using the *Worst Case Scenario* technique, I asked myself what would happen if I took a pottery class, something that I definitely would not excel in. I looked at my fear of being laughed at, fear of being thought stupid, fear of what my family and others would think, fear that I would be the worst one in the class, and general humiliation at not being one of the best. These thoughts looked silly to me after a while as I remembered these words of wisdom, " What others think about you is none of your business."

As a result, I signed up for a pottery class at a local adult education facility and tried to look invisible. We all sat around long tables and made things out of clay. I made a couple of hideous hand built baskets and some colorful Christmas ornaments using cookie cutters. The most exciting thing about this experience was that I had a wonderful time and made new friends. No one seemed to care what anyone else did. There was no criticism, just fun.

This occurrence shook up my belief that if I can't do something really well, there is little point in doing it. A number of years later I was able to overcome some lingering doubts about my artistic ability and took a class called Beads, Beads, Beads. I figured that if I could string beads in Kindergarten, most likely I could do the same thing as an adult without embarrassing myself. That class changed my life. I discovered that I actually had a sense of color and design and embarked on a wonderful hobby that led to making and selling the necklaces I created. I dare you to do something you've been putting off because you know you won't be great at it. I guarantee that you won't be struck by lightning.

93
--

The more you question your behavior and your beliefs, the more you will be able to understand the origins of your perfectionism and see that you have the choice to change. Use the techniques like, *The Cosmic ATM, Worst Case Scenario,* EFT, and *Send in Your Letter of Resignation* to release the irrational fears that keep you stuck. Soon you will feel more compassionate toward yourself and begin to enjoy life more.

Chapter 9

Digging Up the Roots of Procrastination

Although you may believe that you are free to control your life and steer it in any direction you want, the direction you follow is determined by the decisions you have made as your life has unfolded. With each experience, whether positive or negative, your brain has stored your opinions about who you are and the meaning of your life. Consequently, your choices are dependent on these thoughts. In Chapter 7, you learned how insidious False Beliefs like, Failure is unacceptable, or People will dislike me if I don't do it right, can be. You will never be free of procrastination until you go to the source of those False Beliefs and root out their origins.

False Beliefs are created as a result of living with negative Self-fulfilling Prophecies. Self-fulfilling Prophecies are core decisions that are like the software that runs your computer system. Decisions like those listed below became the foundation you built you life upon and led to the choices you made and the actions you took.

Negative beliefs about yourself may include:

  ♦ I am not good enough.

- I am unlovable.
- I am unacceptable.
- I am incompetent.
- I don't belong.
- I am unwanted.
- I am inherently flawed.
- I am powerless.
- I don't matter.
- I am ugly. I am dirty.
- I am worthless.
- It's all my fault.
- I am undeserving.
- I am a victim.
- I am stupid.
- I can't say "no." I can't ask for what I need

Negative beliefs about the world may include:

- Life is hard.
- Life hurts.
- There is no justice in the world
- There is no love in the world.
- Life is dangerous.
- The world is against me.
- I am alone in the world.
- I can't trust God/the Universe to protect me.

Shakespeare said that the world is a stage and people are actors on that stage. Each of us is the star of our own play, some comic and some tragic. When you were very, very young, you decided whether you were good, smart, lovable, and capable, or bad, dumb and a loser. You also decided whether the world was frightening, beautiful, challenging, welcoming or hard and dangerous. Those judgments were assumed to be the *Truth*. As a result, you are living according to those beliefs and behaving in ways that keep you from feeling good about yourself. This is what we call a life script. You wrote yours a long time ago, so long ago that you don't even remember, or, if you do remember making those decisions about yourself and the world, you've grown so used to the way you walk through life, dragging your feet, that it feels natural.

Now it's time to learn how to erase these negative Self-fulfilling Prophecies so you can create and live with new positive beliefs about yourself and rewrite a script free of procrastination. In order to accomplish this you will need to investigate the *level beyond awareness*, the place that holds your history and memories, especially those that were stressful and unpleasant. The conclusions you arrived at about yourself, in an attempt to come to terms with those events, are still at work in your present life and are causing you to procrastinate. If you suffer from problems with depression, or other serious mental health problems or are already working with a mental health professional, your therapist can help you explore these issues.

The World as You Know It

The idea that *I am worthless* may lead you to keep recreating the despair and disregard you felt as a child without realizing it. You may even keep disrespecting yourself as an adult by putting off going to the dentist, eating right, or taking medication when it is prescribed. By procrastinating, you can miss out on wonderful opportunities or relationships.

Believing that *there is no justice in the world* may culminate in a life where you allow yourself to continue to be abused by others in your family, relationships and on the job. You may also create a pattern in your life that *everything is my fault* and believe that you are impaired, stupid or bad and deserve punishment. You might find that no matter what you attempt, you feel like a helpless victim.

If your core belief is that *there is no love in the world,* you may go through life as a seeker of approval, people pleaser, martyr, or person whose actions reflect the idea that you are never good enough and you don't deserve love, success, or happiness. You may fall in love with or go to work for someone who continues to discount or criticize you. Your delaying behaviors then prove that you are unlovable. I have also come across people who started out in life with experiences that taught them that *life is dangerous.* Some of these depressed people become losers because they are unconsciously telling themselves that they are better off not being here at all or that life sucks so why even bother.

There are three ways that Self-fulfilling Prophecies are created.

♦ Some procrastinators receive commands or commandments from the authority figures in childhood. Their words feel as if they have been handed down from God. They must be obeyed without question, or else!

♦ Others create their own prophecies as a result of trying to rationalize life events.

♦ The third way is through our earliest experiences in utero, at birth or in infancy.

Dr. Wendy Anne McCarty, researcher and author in the new field called Primary Psychology, maintains, "Our earliest experiences can hold the key to recognizing and healing our current limiting and debilitating life patterns."

Commands and Commandments

People are not born procrastinators. It is a behavior that results from the ways that we react to our survival instincts.

A Command That Back-Fired

Burt was a graduate school graduate who simply couldn't find a steady job. He kept putting off going on interviews and found many excuses to remain unemployed. Finally, his girlfriend threatened to end their relationship if he didn't overcome his procrastination.

It turned out that Burt had received a command from his parents that caused him to stay stuck because of the way he interpreted their words. They were really loving people and thought they were encouraging him when they drilled this mantra into his head, "Someday someone is going to come along and give you your big break." Burt, a good and loving son, believed his parents.

Now he was waiting for that to happen. Since he had to wait for the unknown benefactor to open the door to success, he was powerless to do anything for himself or it would be a betrayal of his parents' command. Therefore, Burt had to keep himself from moving forward. Without recognizing what he was doing, he created the Self-fulfilling Prophecy: *I can't do it myself.*

Tapping helped him realize that he had misread his parents' intent. He had been successful in grad school and had many talents and abilities. Once he discarded his negative prophecy he was free to make things happen by himself.

Can you think of some of the commandments that still control
your life and lead you to fail?
Make a list of some of them and remember where they came
from. Then use EFT saying,

Even though, _____(Person's name) commanded me to
_____, and following that decree has caused me pain,
I am now freeing myself from having to make it come true.

People Won't Like You

One of the most harmful commandments is: People won't like
you if.... Sometimes this commandment is straightforward.
People won't like you if you are fat. People won't like you
if you talk back. People won't like you if you are too smart.
People won't like you if you look different. The statement,
you'll never amount to much, is both a criticism and a
command to not succeed. Hidden within it is the implied
commandment, People won't like you unless you are
successful! These unloving comments might cause someone to
give up trying or to procrastinate in order to delay the negative
prediction from coming true.

Cursed Forever
The *people won't like you if* . . . curse explains why Joel
procrastinated for most of his adult life about public
speaking and then had an anxiety attack when he attempted
teaching for the first time. When he was growing up, Joel's
abusive mother often warned him "People won't like you if
you stand out!" Although Joel was an expert in his field and
wanted to share his knowledge with others, he kept putting
it off. Finally, he decided to white knuckle it and agreed to
give a class at a community center. He reported that when
he stood up in front of the small group his voice suddenly
gave out. "I could feel my mother's hands around my throat,

choking me," he said. "I remembered her words."

Joel's body re-experienced the fear exactly as though it were happening again. In this case, his mother's prophecy took hold of him to make it come true. As a result of mother's threat, Joel's childhood decision was to avoid putting himself in any situation where he might stand out and be vulnerable to the judgment of others.

Joel had to address this specific memory as well as many other ways his mother's angry outbursts caused him to avoid calling attention to himself in other areas of his life. Psychotherapy and EFT helped him realize that he was still living his life as dictated by a ghost, and he finally freed himself of her curses.

How important is it what other people think? What does "what will people think" really mean? Most likely those "people" whose opinions count are members of your family and anyone else you have given the power to criticize you. I bet you can add them up on the fingers of both hands or maybe only one hand. How many of those people have video cameras pointed at you to see your every move? How many of those people have the time or interest to notice what you are wearing, what you are eating, if you made your bed, paid your bills, finished painting the living room, cleaned out your garage, or made any mistakes today?

When you obsess about what others think, you create a life of bondage to outside validation. A writer who was invited to do a book signing in his hometown procrastinated about accepting the invitation. Going home was terrifying. His fear was what people would think. I asked him who *they* were. His list contained less than ten people, mostly relatives and friends of his parents.

Using EFT he dealt with this by tapping, "Even though I am scared to show my face in my hometown because of what *they* will think, I am exploring this fear now," "Even though one hundred people in town might like my work, what will happen if my family and parents' friends don't, I am tapping about that now." Soon he saw how irrational his fear was and acknowledged that his parents' friends had always liked and supported him and would most likely continue to think of him as a talented person.

Break free now by using EFT to liberate yourself.

- ◆ Even though I worry about what _____ (name of person) thinks about me, I am tapping on that now.

- ◆ Even though I fear _____'s (name of person) disapproval, I deeply accept myself.

- ◆ Even though my worst fear is that I will not live up to _____'s (name of person) expectations, about _____, I am lovable and capable.

Know the Rules

Another implied set of rules goes with the phrase; *you are just like so-and-so.* When Mom tells you that you are just like your Father, does it mean that you are a good athlete or a slob who never puts things away? If you were named after someone in the family, do you feel beholden to take on their characteristics?

Fear of Dying Young

My friend Chuck was named after his beloved uncle. Chuck procrastinated about getting into a committed relationship. He attracted many women, but when they pressured for more he broke away and went on to the next one. His uncle Chuck had tragically died in his thirties and Chuck thought that he was going to follow in his uncle's footsteps, so why marry only to hurt someone by dying? His Self-fulfilling Prophecy was, *the good die young*. After Chuck released himself from the fear that his uncle's history had to be repeated he was able to marry and live beyond his thirties.

You turn yourself into a procrastinator or perfectionist when you hold yourself back for fear of being judged because you believe people won't like you if: you speak up, you are too good, you break the rules, you aren't good enough, you aren't perfect, etc. One man confided that if he stopped holding himself back and allowed himself to let all the intelligence and talent he was capable of be known, he would stand out too much and people would crucify him as they did Jesus. A deity did not hand down these harmful commandments. They are simply the opinions of a bunch of people like you, many of whom are dead and gone. They only hold power over you in your mind.

Tragic Scripts

Dr. Robert Scaer, a researcher and specialist in treating trauma maintains that any type of negative life event that occurs when the person is in a state of relative helplessness can produce the same neurophysiological changes in the brain as those that occur in combat, rape or abuse. He believes that what makes a life event become a trauma isn't the nature of the threat as much as the degree of helplessness the victim fears plus that person's history of other trauma.

Recovery From Abusive Past

Nick was the son of a teenaged unwed mother who later married a man who resented him. Nick's inability to follow through on his plans and promises lost him jobs and friends. He used EFT to de-fuse his painful childhood memories of

103

--

physical and emotional abuse, challenge his fears, and look at his procrastination using statements like:

♦ Even though my mother made what was fun into hard work, I love and accept myself.

♦ Even though my stepfather's harsh rules stopped me from having fun when I was growing up, I am letting go of my anger now.

♦ Even though I didn't feel safe with my stepfather's rage, I survived and I am safe now.

♦ Even though I have many unhappy and unpleasant memories, I am willing to release the pain now.

Many of our Self-fulfilling Prophecies bring us misery and pain because we unwittingly keep re-living them. Here are examples of Self-fulfilling Prophecies that lead to tragic scripts.

♦ My life is about neglect.
♦ My life is about being never good enough.
♦ My life is about being unlovable.
♦ My life is about when I need you, you are never there.
♦ My life is about life sucks and I have to take it.
♦ My life is about pleasing others.
♦ My life is about being invisible.

Therefore, I am supposed to be: abused, blamed, treated like a victim, a loser, bad, disgusting, unlovable, or dead.

The Road To Discovery
Brigitte, a single woman, was molested from ages four to fifteen, and thought it was her fault because she was bad. At the age of 45, this college graduate never earned enough money to have much comfort in her life. She read many self-help books and went to support groups, yet kept putting off taking action that would move her toward a better income.

She was very frustrated because nothing she had done seemed to work. She was unaware that her answer lay in the *level beyond awareness*, her unconscious mind.

When Brigitte used EFT to explore her frustration and procrastination she discovered that one of her False Beliefs was that others would try to take advantage of her and might not like her if she was a financial success. She continued tapping until she uncovered her basic Self-fulfilling Prophecy, *bad things happen to me after something good happens*.

Continued tapping helped Brigitte see the connection between the experiences of her childhood molestation and her procrastination. The first time she was molested by her uncle was on the night of her fourth birthday. No wonder she believed that bad things happen to her after something good happens. She was very young and trusted her uncle. She had received birthday presents and cake, and then her happy day was ruined. She continued to be sexually abused by her uncle and others until she was fifteen. It is hard to imagine the degree of helplessness she endured and the fear of being overwhelmed and mistreated over and over again.

The adult Brigitte finally saw that her four-year-old brain had decided two things, *Bad things happen to me after something good happens*, and *I am bad and I deserve to be punished*. When Brigitte tapped, she saw that she had become addicted to the pain of not having comfort, support, safety, and love. She said, "I'm afraid to let it all go. My pain protects me so it won't happen again." All her excuses were rationalizations that allowed her to continue to push away the possibility of financial security and stay true to her prophecy.

Back to the Very Beginning

There is a new field of psychology that deals with the experiences human beings have from conception through the first year of life. That field focuses on the prenatal and perinatal period and is called Primary Psychology. We were all affected by events that occurred in our parents' lives at conception and the event of our birth. Although our mother's physical and emotional state can have an influence on the baby before birth, we have no idea that it happened since these early experiences are held as implicit memories below the level of our conscious awareness. All of that laid the groundwork for the blueprint of our lives, and still influences how we cope as adults. Amazingly, these early wounds can lead to procrastination.

Dr. Wendy Anne McCarty, maintains that during pregnancy babies are more aware than we ever imagined. They are always responding to what is coming in through the umbilical cord and also from mother's energy state. At this time, they begin to create strategies to deal with what is coming toward them. If the mother is stressed or there is a toxic environment, especially if the mother smokes, drinks or uses drugs, the baby can be overwhelmed with the physical or emotional toxicity. The baby then goes into an adaptive state in order to survive.

If the mother is unhappy with the pregnancy or doesn't want the baby, a conflict arises in both the mother and child. The baby is put into a double bind. It has to participate in the birth journey, but the baby feels like *there is nobody home to protect me*. The baby may disconnect and shut down because of this intolerable wound.

Two patterns that might result from a stressful pregnancy that can lead to procrastination later in life are:

- You avoid what is coming in. You move away from rather than move towards life.
- You numb yourself.

Being Born

Dr. McCarty points out that the experience of our birth is the major imprint about how we shift from one place to another as we live our life. How an adult procrastinator feels on a subconscious level, at each step of the process of moving forward, may mirror how she moved through the birth process forward into the world. Therefore, it helps when procrastinators ask themselves:

- How do I approach a project?
- How do I feel as I begin it?
- How do I feel as I move forward and things get intense when there is no going back?
- How do I feel as I approach the end of the job?
- What do I expect from the outcome of it?

Unfortunately, our culture interrupts the natural birth process by separating the baby from the mother. Since most babies are born in hospitals, the baby is put in the nursery and not with the mother. Birth and bonding is when we triumphantly celebrate the baby's reunion with mother outside the womb and the joy of the journey into life. When we disrupt this experience of feeling good about the outcome of things, this has an effect on the baby that may show up as problems in adulthood. This separation may influence the procrastination problem.

For instance, if there is a difficult or traumatic birth and then the baby is separated from the mother, there is evidence that it triggers a significant stress response in the baby. This stress state is then imprinted in the baby. Two examples of how a difficult birth experience can relate to procrastination are:

♦ You want to start a project and have a sense of dread and don't know why.

♦ You become excited and mobilized, but in the middle you lose energy, feel dread and don't finish.

It Hurt Too Bad

Phil got in touch with his birth experience where there were many complications, and said, "I never quite finish projects. I get anxious toward the end and I stop." After using EFT he gained an understanding of his procrastination process and stated, "I think I never wanted to feel that way again." The emotional pain of a difficult birth was still held in his unconscious and kept surfacing, much to his frustration. Tapping helped him free himself to be able to complete what he started.

Who Is To Blame?

Another person who discovered that her behavior was rooted in her first weeks of life was Sheila, whose Self-fulfilling Prophecy was, *when I need you, you are never there.* After Sheila's divorce she was left with two small children and a deadbeat ex-husband, Jeff, who couldn't hold a job long enough to pay child support. Sheila was furious with him since she didn't have enough money to make ends meet. She decided to go back to work full time, but couldn't seem to get herself to follow up on this plan. Things got worse and worse. The bill collectors were knocking at the door. Sheila was increasingly stressed as her financial worries mounted and she became sick. She had to apply for aid so her children could get health care.

Sheila didn't want to focus on her procrastination, even though putting off finding a job was adding to her stress. She preferred to rage at Jeff for letting her down and got pleasure being a martyr. As she tapped on her anger with Jeff, for abandoning them financially, this is what came to the surface after she said, "Even though I am furious with Jeff for not following through with his commitment to take care of us, I am doing the best I can."

- He was a lousy husband.
- Husbands are supposed to take care of wives
- My parents wanted me to marry someone who would take care of me.
- My father took care of us.
- My mother was sick when I was born and had to go away for treatment.
- She was supposed to take care of me, but she wasn't there.
- Then she went to work, and my grandma took care of me but she died and left me too.
- Everyone who loves me leaves me!
- My first husband died too and left me.
- They were supposed to take care of me and they didn't.
- How could they leave me like that?
- I'm so angry! Angry! Angry!
- But it wasn't their fault. They couldn't help it.
- They did the best they could.
- I feel so sad for baby Sheila.
- I am not a child any more.
- I have to take care of my own children.

- ♦ I can take care of my children.
- ♦ I will take care of my children.

Unconsciously Sheila had chosen a husband like Jeff who, like her mother, would not be there when she needed him during their marriage and after the divorce. She was just playing out the drama that started right after her birth when her mother, who was ambivalent to begin with about having another baby, had to be sent away for convalescence.

Although she was only a few weeks old and had no recollection of that time, a part of her remembered how it felt to not be taken care of and not bonding with a loving mother. The death of her beloved grandmother a few years later was one of the great losses in her life. Even as an adult, her inner child self still wanted to be taken care of. She expected her husbands to provide the security that her mother owed her and hadn't given. However, her first husband was an unstable man who committed suicide early in their marriage and left her alone again. Jeff's inability to support the family and provide security also made her feel abandoned.

After she saw the way her Self-fulfilling Prophecy had come into being and how she had continued to re-enact it, EFT helped her to clear the yearning of her infancy, the traumas of her grandmother's and first husband's deaths, and release the feelings of grief and loss. Then Sheila stopped expecting Jeff to be reliable and found new ways to provide security for herself and her children.

If you have been told negative stories about your birth, you may want to tap on one or more of these suggestions:

- ♦ Even though it was devastating/frightening/threatening coming into this life, and I wish it had been different, I totally love and accept myself and understand myself.

110

--

- Even though my mother didn't want me and I felt like dying because it was so painful, I survived and I love and accept myself.

- Even though my mother's state during pregnancy caused me stress in the womb, she didn't know that she was doing it, and I survived and am accepting myself now.

- Even though my birth was traumatic and I still have conflict about starting or finishing things, I understand why that could be and forgive all who harmed me although they thought they were doing their best, including myself.

You Done Me Wrong

Brigitte and Sheila made themselves miserable due to the painful prophecies they were keeping alive. Their procrastination was like a temper tantrum because they wanted something that was withheld at birth or early childhood. Sheila thought she was angry with her ex-husband Jeff but she really was still reacting to the wound of not having her mother care for her at birth. Brigitte wanted the safety and nurturing she never had as she was growing up.

Use EFT and tap on any of these sentences after you fill in the blanks, or make up your own about those who let you down (whether accidentally or on purpose).

- (Name of person) How miserable do I have to be for you to feel bad and _____

- (Name of person) How low do I have to sink before you

111
--

will _____

♦ (Name of person) How sick do I have to get before you will _____

♦ (Name of person) How incompetent do I have to act before you will _____

Find the Roots

How can you find out if you were set up to procrastinate as a result of an early experience that you don't remember? One way is to use the *Cosmic ATM technique*. Imagine that you are standing in front of an ATM machine and need to withdraw some information.

1. Think of the feeling you have when you confront the situation or task that you are putting off or not finishing. (dread, anger, sadness, anxiety etc.)

2. Ask the question, how young is the part of me that is feeling this feeling? Take a deep breath and let it out saying, "I don't know."

3. Wait patiently in a relaxed state until you receive an answer. It most likely will be a number but may be a picture or even a voice telling you.

4. Tap on the answer. "Even though something happened to me when I was ___ years old that is still affecting my life and causing me to procrastinate, I am treating that event now."

Perhaps you will want to ask your unconscious mind how young you were when the roots of your procrastination first appeared by using a pendulum or muscle testing as described in Chapter 4. When you find the age it all started, you can ask how many rounds you need to tap to clear the original ordeal. After you tap those rounds, check in with muscle testing or pendulum to ask if you succeeded or if you need to tap some more.

Now you know the whole story about when and where the seeds of procrastination were sown and how to dig them out by the roots. I believe that procrastination is not just a bad habit, but a complex behavior that results from a lifetime of stress and fear and the need to avoid reliving negative experiences of the past. I hope that you can now view your procrastination without judgment but with compassion for yourself.

Chapter 10

Keep Moving Forward

Procrastination is not a disease that can be cured with medication. There is no inoculation for procrastination that will prevent it from recurring. The habit of putting things off is a signal from the unconscious mind, a reminder that you are avoiding facing something. By now you are aware that procrastination is a compulsive reaction that helps you steer clear of situations or relationships that seem threatening or uncontrollable. In this chapter, I will offer you simple suggestions to use when you find yourself falling back into your old habits.

As a result of reading and practicing the exercises described in the previous chapters,

♦ You have learned to become conscious of your anxiety about starting new undertakings.
♦ You are familiar with ways to recognize and treat your negative thoughts and False Beliefs.
♦ You know how to employ EFT to transform your fears and discomforts.
♦ You are aware of what triggers you to pull back from beginning a project or stopping in the middle without completing it.

♦ You have searched out your negative *Self-fulfilling Prophecies.*

♦ You have uncovered and treated the early wounds that created your need to sabotage yourself by procrastinating.

Where do you go from here?

The Daily Workout

Going to the gym every day is a popular pastime for many people to maintain physical fitness. I recommend that you start the day with a three-step mental *Daily Workout* to keep procrastination from recurring. It takes only minutes to perform.

Step One: Tune in to any physical discomfort or stress you are feeling and use EFT to eliminate it in a minute or two. You may start the day with a headache or crankiness due to sleep problems. Perhaps you will use feeling bad as an excuse to not go forward with an endeavor.

Step Two: Think of whatever tasks, chores or projects you are annoyed at not tackling today. Then take one at a time and tap the energy points until you come up with a plan that relieves your anxiety and gets you into action. Remember, you can do this very rapidly.

Step Three: Use EFT to take the edge off any chronic problems that can't be resolved quickly but are causing you ongoing life stress. Give yourself a speedy three round tapping treatment for worry about a loved one, problems with chronic health issues or other compulsions like overeating, drinking or Internet addiction that are often the ways procrastinators tend to distract themselves.

If you don't like this three-step workout, you can create one that works for you. The important thing is to do this every day. I like to tap away my stress in the morning before I start my day, however a client reported that she does it at bedtime to get rid of what has accumulated during the day. Experiment until you find what suits you best.

Other Daily Tools

Another way to deal with daily or ongoing stresses that lead to procrastination is to consult with your Inner Knower by writing to Dear Abby (see Chapter 5). This should not take more than five minutes. Write a paragraph to Abby or your favorite symbolic wise advisor describing what is going on and what the problem is that is leading to avoidance behaviors. Ask for advice. Next, turn the paper over and write, "Dear _____ (your name), I read your letter with great interest. You are a good and worthy person and deserve success and happiness." Keep your pen moving and let the words flow out without trying to think the problem through. Suggestions and resolutions will come forth.

In Chapter 4, I showed you how George used the *Be Your Own Best Friend* technique to get to the heart of his problem. He used EFT and talked out loud to as if he was talking to a friend. He said something different at each energy point, going round and round until he reached a satisfactory resolution to his problem. If you can't move past a negative situation or emotion, do what George did and see what happens.

Occasionally a procrastinator can't understand what it is that she is really avoiding. Using the *Worst Case Scenario* technique helped one woman discover that clearing the piles of junk that had built up in her laundry room was not the real problem. By interrogating herself over and over with the question, "What am I afraid is waiting for me if I finish this project?" she found that her procrastination was keeping her safe from another more demanding job that was waiting for her once that was done. Another student at one of my workshops found that it wasn't even the job after the present task that he was anxious about, it was the third project down the line that he feared! Keep this in mind when you want to quit.

Decisions, Decisions, Decisions

Procrastinators often put things off because they don't know how to make decisions and keep taking their decisions back. I stopped shopping with my husband years ago because he could never make up his mind. He is one of those people who are trim with a perfect average body. Everything he tries on fits him perfectly. I have stood by and watched him try a dozen pairs of slacks or jackets. To my eyes, he looked great in every one, but he refused to choose. After tramping through store after store and agonizing about making up his mind, he often went home empty handed. It drove me up the wall to witness his indecision.

What is behind the hesitation to take the plunge? It all boils down to fear. There is something about making a commitment that seems to paralyze the person. Of course, the easiest way to break the deadlock of indecision is to use the *Be Your Own Best Friend* technique and talk about what you are thinking that is keeping you from making the decision as you tap.

Making decisions can become easy when you follow these guidelines.

1. Define your goal
2. List your choices
3. Focus on your priorities
4. Match your choices to your priorities
5. Make a decision

Let's imagine that you are buying a pair of pants. Your goal would be: purchase a pair (or more if that is your goal) of pants. Once you are in the store, you have many choices. You can choose from different styles, different materials and different colors or patterns. Look through what is available and see what attracts you. Priorities refer to your main concerns in purchasing this piece of clothing. Are you shopping for pants to wear to a social event, for everyday wear, to wear when you are doing chores? Is it important to buy something that is washable or is it OK to buy a dry clean only garment? Do you have a preference about color, style or fit? What is your price range? All of these must be taken into consideration.

Once you have narrowed the field down, match the pants you are trying to decide about with your priorities and see what happens. If you want pants for everyday wear and have small children or pets that can spill or shed on you, you may not want something that must be dry-cleaned. For many people, the price is definitely one of their main concerns. Taking all these guidelines into consideration, choose the pants that fit your goal.

After you have decided what to purchase, discard any notion about the others. Do not take back your decision! This is the hardest part for many procrastinators. They second-guess themselves. If you are tempted to take back your decision, use EFT immediately to eliminate your doubts and understand your self-sabotaging behavior, or try the *Worst Case Scenario* technique, asking what is the worst thing that might happen if you purchase these pants.

Emergency First Aid Kit

If you follow these six steps any time you feel stuck and can't move forward with a goal or project, you will see immediate results. You may want to copy this brief guide onto an index card and keep it handy on your desk or hang it on your refrigerator.

Quick Guide To Get Going

1. **What is my goal?** Name the task, job, or project you want to finish. Check that it is smart. Is it specific, reasonable, attainable and is this the right time to attempt it?

2. **What excuses am I using to avoid completing it**? Say or write down all the excuses you can think of that you are tempted to use to stop yourself from starting, going on with or completing this endeavor. Remind yourself that excuses don't count. Cross them out.

3. **What is the worst thing that might happen if I complete it?** Quiz yourself and keep pushing to discover what your fear thoughts are. Then use EFT when you get to the heart of it.

4. **What belief is stopping me cold**? Review the five main False Beliefs: Failure is unacceptable, People will dislike me if I don't do it right, Success is dangerous, I'm afraid of what the future holds, and I don't want to. Use EFT on any or all the beliefs that are sabotaging you.

5. **How young was I when I decided this was the truth, and what was going on**? Use the Cosmic ATM procedure or try out self muscle testing/pendulum/ ideomotor finger methods to discover the age. Use EFT to free yourself from the negative results of that memory.

6. **What have I decided to do?** Take action now.

You now have all the tools you need to become a former procrastinator. If you relapse and find yourself procrastinating again, instead of giving up on yourself or telling yourself that this book didn't work, do a post mortem examination of the incident. Dissect your behavior to notice what happened and what didn't happen. Look for the familiar patterns. Was this act of procrastination similar to or different from your behavior in the past? Even though you didn't stop yourself from stopping, you can learn something from each step back that will help you to not repeat it the next time.

Commit yourself to live your life consciously, having compassion for yourself and the unhealed wounds that may still affect you. Remember that you have a secret weapon, EFT, which can eliminate anxiety and fear from the past and the present. Self-fulfilling Prophecies can be extremely strong and usually have become a familiar way of being. Congratulate yourself each time you discover that a bit of negative or self-demeaning thinking still remains. It means that you are continuing to hunt down and dig up the roots of your procrastination.

As the days go by, I hope you will remember to use the new tools you have learned. If you don't then you might want to re-read the section about resisting change in Chapter 4. Do you have any blocking beliefs that are still holding you back? I hope you have the courage to face them and tap them away so you can continue on your path to success.

Chapter 11

Advice to Family and Friends

It is difficult and often painful to watch those we love or care for do something that hurts them. The worst part is when they do it over and over and don't seem to be able to stop despite the negative consequences of their actions. My husband was a world-class procrastinator when I met him, but he has changed greatly thanks to taking my classes and having me as his coach. I can speak from experience since I have lived with him up close and personal for over thirty years "for better or worse."

Non-procrastinators may be puzzled and annoyed by procrastinators. As a marriage counselor I am used to hearing one partner complain, "If only he/she would _____ things would be fine." What this really means is, "If only my parent/child/spouse/friend could be just like me." Nevertheless, the procrastinator in your life will never be just like you. And it often doesn't help to tell someone how to let go of his or her problem. Like all of us, procrastinators are capable of change, but no one likes to be criticized or bullied.

Even when we think we know someone, there can be an aspect of him or her we need to explore and understand. Every procrastinator has a reason for procrastinating, and that reason may be hidden. It is up to you, as the loved one of a procrastinator to approach them in a compassionate manner while also taking care of yourself and your needs.

My husband is a true Renaissance man. He is a masterful do-it-yourselfer, an artist, painter, woodworker, fixer of appliances, computers, cars, and you name it. I often give thanks for all he does, but it isn't all he does that is the problem. It is when he gets around to starting or finishing all he does that used to cause my blood pressure to rise.

The Thanksgiving Story

One memorable Thanksgiving morning, a few hours before our family was coming for dinner, my husband left the house. He ran out to the store to buy matching folding chairs. At that time, we were living in a house that had a huge kitchen but no dining room, hence no dining room furniture that included a matching table and chairs.

I was fuming because I needed his help with other preparations. His need for things to look perfect was bugging me, the former perfectionist. I went into the guest bathroom to admire the new wallpaper we had put up, and make sure the guest soap and towels were in place. Then I glanced down at the floor. He had not replaced the molding along the bottom of the walls after hanging the wallpaper a few months before. There was a gaping empty area along each wall. I was confused. How could he spend a couple of hours on a national holiday trying to find an open store that sold chairs but not care that the bathroom was incomplete and far from perfect?

I took a deep breath and got on with my preparations. It seemed obvious to me that my husband's behavior was motivated by the fear of what people will think, but which people? I couldn't figure out why he was more concerned with the chairs than the bathroom molding. At the end of the day, after everyone had gone, I told him that I was perplexed by his behavior. "I can't understand why you drove around like a madman trying to buy matching chairs, yet you weren't embarrassed by all the people who went into the unfinished bathroom today."

I asked my husband what he was afraid would happen if the chairs didn't match. Who would care? What would happen if someone did? He explained that his mother used to try to put on airs to impress people. Since she didn't think she was good enough, she had to put on a facade of being perfect. I assumed from his story that the chairs were what people would see immediately as they sat down to the feast, but not everyone would go into the bathroom.

I asked what else caused him worry. He couldn't come up with an answer except that it would displease his mother. "But she's dead!" I reminded him. "Was she perfect?" It was evident that his mother's need for approval still reverberated through his psyche so many years later. Even though he was a grown man and knew better, his amygdala triggered emotional flashes about things looking perfect when company was coming and getting the approval of others. He turned into a scared child at these moments.

When I was growing up, we lived in an apartment without a dining room. I recall many happy holiday meals when we would open a table in the living room and pull up any available chairs, even the piano bench. Nobody minded. They remembered the happy times and my mother's wonderful cooking. My husband was influenced by his mother's disapproval. I was influenced by my mother's lack of worry about what people might think. It is interesting how two people can have entirely different reactions to the same event, in this case Thanksgiving dinner at home. My husband and I have very different histories, yet we tend to assume that the other person should think and feel as we do. Once we were able to share our stories, I felt great sympathy for what he had lived through. It helps to remind myself of this when he does something I can't understand and I feel the frustration start to rise.

The History Lesson

If you and the procrastinator in your life have incidents like this, the first step is to take time for a History Lesson.

- ◆ Calm yourself with slow breaths or EFT to eliminate your anger or frustration.
- ◆ Create an attitude of inquiry. Think of yourself as an investigator rather than an interrogator.
- ◆ Gently ask the procrastinator for information about what motivated their behavior that puzzles or angers you.
- ◆ See if you can encourage the person to look back into his or her history to discover who they are still trying to please or appease.
- ◆ Look into your own history to compare your experiences, how you were treated and what decisions you made.
- ◆ If possible, ask the procrastinator to use EFT, about the early memory or fear.

Refer the procrastinator to *the tyranny of the shoulds* in Chapter 5 to revisit the discussion about the people in his life whose behavior modeled, "Do as I say and not as I do." Encourage the procrastinator to explain why those people were appointed by the deity to be His representative on earth to judge, jeer or punish. What qualifications made those people worthy to judge your loved one or friend? The procrastinator can also choose to do some of the exercises described in Chapter 9 to move beyond the untrue commandments he or she is still bowing down to.

The Worst Case Scenario

Getting to know your friend or partner is an ongoing endeavor. I am constantly learning about the complexities of human behavior from my husband. There was the time when he was having computer trouble and spent five or more hours a day for almost a week trying to fix things while I looked on impatiently, telling myself that it would have been easier to call a computer repair person to get it working again.

I finally asked my husband to use the *Worst Case Scenario* technique. I asked him to ponder what he was afraid would happen if he let someone else fix the computer. I kept asking until a realization emerged that clarified his actions. This is a simple way to get a peek inside the brain of a procrastinator and gain empathy and understanding.

"What's the worst thing that would happen if you let someone fix your computer?" I asked. My husband got in touch with a strong feeling of helplessness. I suggested that he use EFT to explore this awareness. He said, "Even though I feel helpless at the thought of someone fixing my computer for me, I am exploring this feeling now." This is what he discovered:

- ◆ If I let someone else do it, I will be helpless.
- ◆ I am afraid of being helpless.
- ◆ I was helpless when I was little.
- ◆ My mother abandoned me when I was 2 years old.
- ◆ I was powerless to change anything.
- ◆ I couldn't trust her. I couldn't trust anyone.
- ◆ I had no power over my life.
- ◆ I had to take care of myself
- ◆ I had to be independent and resourceful to be safe.

Once I heard his story my irritation disappeared. When you use this technique with the procrastinators in your life, you can suggest that they use EFT to heal the past experiences or treat the harmful beliefs that are holding them back.

Better Late than Never?

Another issue that causes unhappiness in relationships is how people use time. My husband and I have different definitions of the word "now." I say that now means *immediately*. His *now* is somewhat different. I never know from day to day whether *now* means in a few minutes or hours. Sometimes it means in a day or two. The cartoon, Pickles, drawn by Brian Crane, depicts the humor in the daily life of a retired couple. In one of my favorite strips, the wife is upset because her husband said he would do something she requested ASAP (As Soon As Possible). Her husband then explains that to him ASAP stands for After September, April Probably.

I like to say that my husband lives in Cosmic Time. Although he usually gets places on time, he leaves preparation until the last minute. I, on the other hand, worry about whether we will meet traffic or not, find a parking place, or miss the first act, so I like to factor in the unexpected. Who is right? This is an area where people will constantly be triggering each other. How can they accept someone they love or respect and are aggravated by at the same time?

Each latecomer has his own story. Sandy was fed up with her husband Gary. Like my husband, he was often late to things or waited until the last minute and barely squeaked by. Gary sold insurance. One day he was running late for an appointment with a prospective customer and realized that he had misplaced the address and driving instructions. He started running around the house, half dressed, trying to find the piece of paper with the information on it. Sandy noticed that he was wasting time and suggested that he call the person and reveal that he had misplaced the address. It would only take a minute. Gary angrily yelled that he might have it on his email and went for the computer. Sandy felt concern since she thought he might make a bad impression if he was late. The more she tried to reason with him, the more he yelled at her. Finally, she gave up and walked away. He eventually phoned and got the address and directions, but both of them were left with upset feelings toward each other.

I advised Sandy to wait a few days until this incident was past and then, when they were in a pleasant mood, discuss it with Gary by trying the *Worst Case Scenario* technique. When Sandy asked Gary what he was afraid would happen if he had phoned right away instead of taking so much time looking for the lost scrap of paper, he explained that he could visualize the paper where he had written the address and knew it was there, therefore he had to find it. Sandy asked again, "What were you afraid would happen if you stopped looking and phoned? It seemed so simple and efficient to me." Gary thought for a minute and said sternly, "Seeking help from others is a confession of failure. It is not knowing what I *should* have known, and *there's no excuse for that!*"

Sandy was surprised at the vehemence of those words. "Who talked to you like that when you were growing up?" she inquired. She wasn't surprised when Gary explained how his father had been highly critical of him and was physically abusive at times. Gary continued, "If I don't know, something terrible will happen to me." This was Gary's Self-fulfilling Prophecy. It lay behind many of his avoidance behaviors.

Sandy thought of her upbringing and compared it to Gary's. Her family hadn't treated her like that. The idea that a person is supposed to automatically know something they don't know, and will be punished for not knowing, was incomprehensible and ridiculous to her. It didn't make sense, but it explained a lot about her husband. In psychology, we call Gary's father's behavior "crazy making."

Having a close relationship with another person can be compared to going to a movie with a friend where both of you have entirely different responses to the same film. One person is moved to tears while the other may be bored stiff. That is what Sandy understood after hearing her husband's story. Instead of reacting to Gary when he didn't do things her way, the "simple and obvious" way, she could remind herself that what seemed innocent and neutral to one of them was fraught with danger to the other. They could both continue to share their histories and to do the *Worst Case Scenario* technique when these moments occurred. In addition, they could each use EFT to transform their reactions to situations and to each other.

Who Are You?

It is vital to stop expecting the other to be your clone. My husband will never be me, nor do I want him to be. Remember the best selling book that explained that women are from Venus and men are from Mars? Well, differences in how we think and act are not just divided according to the sexes. Each of us comes into the world with certain characteristics that will be ours for life. For instance, eye color doesn't change, and once we achieve our full height that is that, no matter what. We each have a different blueprint.

We are born with other qualities that determine how we travel through life. These traits form our disposition or temperament.

This usually remains unchanging and doesn't alter. For example, people seem to have the tendency to be either introverts or extroverts from the beginning. I am extroverted. I like to be in front of a class or audience. Others, who are more introverted, like my husband would rather die than speak in public. I can't imagine that I could ever transform myself into an introvert, no matter how hard I try. At the same time, introverts can't imagine themselves being more outgoing in a crowd. Which are you? Can you imagine yourself acting the opposite? Then you can appreciate how different a procrastinator is from a non-procrastinator.

Another set of attributes that often causes difficulties in relationships has to do with whether a person is Goal-oriented or Process-oriented. Goal-oriented people have their eyes on the target and do what is necessary to get there. They like a planned and organized approach to life and prefer to have things settled. Process-oriented people tend to have a flexible and spontaneous approach to life and prefer to keep their options open. They are prone to smell the roses along the way. They are more interested in the journey than the conclusion. When a Process-oriented person is in a relationship with a Goal-oriented person, the fireworks can fly.

One of the greatest tests in relationships is how to accept other people if they have a different temperament from you, don't think like you, don't view the world like you, and certainly don't act like you. This is especially true when one is a procrastinator or perfectionist. My husband is Process-oriented and tends to become distracted from his goals. He goes off on tangents while I steadfastly move forward.

If you are the friend, co-worker or spouse of someone who has a very different disposition, remember this advice: You can't get milk from a bull! Ask yourself what you need to do to stop reacting. One of the solutions I have come up with is to accept the other person as he or she is and acknowledge that we both have strengths and limitations. I capitalize on my strengths by doing the things I am best at like organization and follow-through. I admire my husband's strengths and encourage him to use them.

What Is Best for You?

Over the years, I have perceived that procrastinators tend to underestimate how long it will take for them to complete a project. After observing my husband I no longer delude myself that it should take less time since I am a Goal-oriented person and he isn't. We use time differently. He always finishes what he begins, but it is in his time, not mine. I must admit that there have been times when I let it get the best of me. I have ranted and raised my voice, however since I learned to use EFT, I take time to tap about my reaction and resolve my disappointment as well as deepen my understanding and acceptance of our differences. I always tap until I reach a feeling of peace and love. Then I share my discoveries with my husband so he can understand what made me react and we both can let go of any residue of anger toward each other.

As a non-procrastinator, you have to take care of yourself physically and emotionally. We each have what I like to call an "emotional comfort zone." That means that there is a certain amount of chaos that you can handle each day. It may vary from day to day depending on your stress. Therefore, although my husband can do many things well, there are times I hire another person to do that job since I need to have it finished sooner that he can complete it.

Brotherly Love

Victoria learned this lesson the hard way. She wanted to repaint the inside of her home and asked her brother to do that job for her since he was very handy. Unfortunately, he was also a procrastinator. They had agreed that he would come at 8:30 AM every day, but most of the time he showed up at noon. She assumed that he would complete one room at a time, but instead he pushed all the furniture to the center of each room, primed the walls and then painted them one at a time. The entire house was in disarray. At one point, he left town to go on a vacation and left things as they were. As the job dragged on and on Victoria became extremely stressed and had trouble sleeping. Finally, she became ill and had to see a doctor. The first thing the doctor asked her after hearing her symptoms was if she had been under any undo stress lately! After this traumatic experience, she decided that although she loved her brother, she would not hire him in the future.

Look at Yourself

You will have to make the decision for yourself about how much you want to tolerate when you are dealing with a procrastinator or perfectionist. If you become angry, anxious, or ill, use the Be *Your Own Best Friend* tapping technique and talk our loud to yourself as if you were discussing your unhappiness with a friend.

An Aggravated Mom

When Barbara started to feel upset because her daughter Toni was procrastinating she began to tap about her distress and discovered that she was fearful even though she was not the person who would bear the consequence of the behavior. She was afraid that if Toni didn't follow through, Barbara would be embarrassed because she was associated with her daughter and would be judged too. Tapping helped Barbara decide that what others thought about her was just their opinion and none of her concern. She released her daughter to bear the consequences of her own actions.

If you tap on your frustration or anger, you may find out that you are worrying that the fall-out of the procrastinator's behavior might affect you in a negative way. Could their inaction keep you from finishing a project, cause you to miss a show, or disappoint a friend? Like Barbara, you may learn that another's problem is not yours.

She Can't Stop Him

Sandy feared that when her husband Gary was running late he might drive too fast and get a ticket or have an accident. She also fantasized that it could happen when she was in the car with him when they were late to a social engagement or even trying to make it to a movie on time. This underlying fear increased her aggravation when she saw that he was rushing and out of control.

After she tapped, she decided that she could handle these moments in different ways. She could tell him that she felt unsafe when he started to drive recklessly with her in the car and request that he calm down. She might say, "I notice that you are in a rush and I don't feel safe so I'll drive," or she might even decide to take her own car and meet him at the destination.

Small acts of procrastination can be extremely irritating. Some people hate it when their partner or roommate "forgets" to put the top on the toothpaste. My annoyance is when my husband "forgets" about putting his spoon in the sink after stirring his coffee. Year in and year out, I have found the spoon on the counter after he has left the house. Finally, I took my own advice and tapped. I realized that a few years ago he had surgery for a very serious condition. What if he had died and I was alone? If that had happened, I would miss his quirks. They would dwindle in importance. Tapping helped put it in perspective.

Now when he acts like his own dear Process-oriented self I remind myself of that and also remind myself that he has to live with my Goal-oriented ways that drive him nuts. Once, in a fit of remorse about my need to have things my way, I asked him how he put up with me controlling everything. He replied, "I just let you." The man is a saint!

Once you grasp the idea that all procrastinators are doing the best they can at that moment, as you are too, I hope that you will be able to accept them. Don't set tests for other people that you know they can't pass. Procrastinators suffer from a compulsion to not do that is triggered by thoughts, beliefs, and Self-fulfilling Prophecies based in the past that are still part of their brain's program. Instead of acting critical, punishing or scoffing, encourage your friends to look at their patterns and use EFT to help them successfully change their behavior. In addition, it will help you to look at your reactions and take action to prevent anger or anxiety that will affect the relationship.

Appendix I

Brain Chemistry Malfunctions

Matt, an experienced do-it-yourselfer, could fix anything. Months after Matt and his wife Laura decided it was time to replace the old linoleum in the storage room with new vinyl tiles, an easy job for someone with his experience, he worked all weekend and accomplished over 90% of it. Although there was only a bit left to do, Matt became sidetracked when he and Laura started to plan for renovating their bathroom. They worked together to shop for and hire people to put in new counters, fixtures and flooring. The unfinished storage room floor was forgotten. Matt turned his attention to next challenge, repaint the bathroom to match the new color scheme.

Meanwhile Matt remembered that he had promised to refinish the dining room table and chairs so the following weekend he got involved working on one of the chairs and continued during his free time until that was done. With another five chairs and the table still waiting, Matt's neighbor asked him to help with a computer problem he was experiencing. That took a few more evenings. More projects seemed to pop up and Matt kept busy with everything else except the refinishing project. Another month went by with the rest of the dining room set still waiting, and the bathroom walls untouched. Now Matt began talking about replacing the faucets in the bathrooms. He had purchased new faucets the year before that were still sitting on a shelf in the garage.

Attention Deficit Disorder

Eventually most of these tasks will be completed. It is just that Matt has trouble getting started with things, is easily distracted, has difficulty completing, goes from one thing to another before the first is completed, seems disorganized, can't keep track of goals, supplies or time, and doesn't seem aware that he is demonstrating any of these behaviors.

These are some of the signs of Attention Deficit Hyperactivity Disorder. ADHD is not limited to children. Adults with ADHD symptoms or behaviors find that it affects their lives at work, within the family, and in social relationships. Distractibility, impulsivity and hyperactivity are the most common features of this problem. ADHD seems to be caused by biological factors that influence chemical activity in certain parts of the brain. The types of symptoms and their severity will vary from person to person; however, chronic procrastination may be related to ADHD.

Some people with ADHD find that medication can help to normalize brain activity. If you identify with Matt, I recommend that you seek evaluation by a health professional that specializes in ADHD, find counseling or coaching and look into support groups to learn coping skills and adaptive behaviors. Use your computer to research more about ADHD. ADDitude magazine at *www.attitudemag.com* is worth reading to learn more.

Obsessive Compulsive Disorder (OCD)

Many years ago, I was a psychological "expert" on an episode of the *Montel Williams Show* about people who suffered from various compulsions. Each panelist was accompanied by a relative or loved one who was there supposedly to support the troubled person, but was really expected to criticize and complain. One participant was unable to control her need to have everything organized and orderly. Her obsession was so powerful that when she baby-sat in someone's home, she not only cleaned up dishes and vacuumed but also felt driven to rearrange their furniture. She was not a nuisance; she suffered from Obsessive Compulsive Disorder (OCD).

OCD results from a chemical imbalance in the brain. It is not a sign of mental illness or low intelligence, just a glitch in the brain. This problem is characterized by obsessive, distressing, intrusive thoughts and related compulsions, tasks or rituals that the person creates to allay their anxiety. Some people are plagued by recurrent and persistent thoughts or images. The person tries to ignore or suppress them with another thought or action. He feels driven to perform repetitive behaviors in order to reduce distress or prevent something dreadful from occurring. Those with OCD are aware of the irrationality of the obsession but are unable to overcome it. Some people with OCD must count or double check that things are OK, others can't stop washing their hands or performing rituals to avoid germs.

Another group are clutterers. The World Health Organization lists this condition as one of the top ten most disabling illnesses in terms of lost income and diminished quality of life. One of the women on the Montel Williams Show, Roz, was a pack rat. I will never forget the film they showed of her home. Half the width of the staircase was piled with books and other miscellaneous items on each step. It had become so narrow that a person would have to go up the stairs sideways. The guest room was so completely packed that the door would no longer open. The kitchen was filthy and messy beyond description. Her sister described how horrible this problem was and how upset she was with Roz's inability to take action to clean up and clear out the mess. Poor Roz was not a procrastinator on purpose. She too suffered from a form of Obsessive Compulsive Disorder.

Although many clutterers refer to themselves as hoarders, only a very small percentage of clutterers suffer from the serious psychological condition of hoarding. The woman I met on the Montel Williams Show suffered from that problem and should have been treated by a psychiatrist. Hoarders endure acute anxiety at the thought of discarding anything. In extreme cases, the clutter completely takes over their living space.

Clatterers seem to let things pile up willy-nilly until the mess becomes a problem while hoarders are obsessed about their possessions and feel compelled to collect. Hoarders cannot make rational decisions about what is useful and what is not. Some even save garbage or soiled items. After her mother died, a friend of mine was shocked and sickened when she had to go through many years worth of accumulated clutter. She discovered boxes of very expensive sets of fine china along with decaying bags of garbage.

Another extreme hoarder who wasn't aware of the extent of her problem was Florence, a delightful woman who kept collecting things, especially stuffed animals. There were so many things on her bed that there was no place to put them when she went to sleep so she had gotten used to sleeping on half the bed and never changed the sheets. Once she started de-cluttering, she brought me two small swatches of cloth to look at. One was dark beige and the other white with pastel stripes. She explained that when she finally addressed the problem of her bed and stripped it, the part of the sheet below the toys was still white while the side she slept on had turned brown!

The Symbolism of Clutter

Clutter can be symbolic. Some clutterers amass "things" because they experienced terrible deprivation in the past due to living during times of war or extreme poverty. They are unconsciously protecting themselves from the possibility it could happen again. Eighty year-old Molly's refrigerator was filled with little packets and bits of leftovers that were often green and moldy. She grew up during the great depression of the 1930's when she was told that it was a sin to waste food. Therefore, she was unable to throw food away.

Another clutterer, Ralph, grew up in a poor family with a father who taught him to "make do" or be thrifty. Ralph couldn't throw old broken machines or tools away because he said, "You never know when you might need them." If you are like Molly or Ralph, you can benefit by tapping on those early memories. Keep tapping until you decide how to deal with your early programming

Cluttering puts people into a double bind. There is comfort in holding onto things, yet the mess builds until the person is overwhelmed and feels helpless, hopeless, like a failure and unworthy. According to Dr. Roland Rotz, a psychologist who specializes in helping clutterers, "The hope of cleaning up makes up for their sense of hopelessness about their lives. Their attachment to things may make up for the emptiness in their lives."

A client who used EFT to explore this realized, "If I clean up I'll have free time and I might have to face things I don't want to face." As she continued to tap, she was able to acknowledge and face some of the things she had been repressing such as fear of aging, loneliness and unresolved memories of childhood abuse.

Walter, a recently retired man, was very depressed about his clutter. I asked him to use EFT and he tapped "Even though I want to give up and die, since I can never get rid of this mess, I know it is the OCD talking and I am doing the best I can." Little by little, he has made great inroads in his home, and now his guest room is free of clutter on the floor, dresser and bed.

It is vital to get past the shame of feeling like a failure and the fear of what people will think it they see the mess. Most clutterers are extremely reluctant to let others help them. Sometimes it is because they are afraid that the helper will throw everything away. Other times it is the fear that the helper will not understand the importance the object has for the clutterer.

Although there may be a lot of junk, there are also objects that symbolize important moments in the clutterer's life. One of the things that helped Amy de-clutter was to look at all the pieces of clothing clogging her closet that were now long out of style and too small and choose just one to represent each era or memorable event. In addition, Amy was in her fifties and still had every notebook from college classes she'd taken more than 25 years earlier. They hadn't been opened in all that time. She chose to keep a copy of her senior honor's paper and toss the rest.

Solutions

When I have a client with OCD who has a clutter problem, I suggest that she tap about her low self-esteem saying, "Even though I hate myself because my house is so messy I won't let anyone in the door, it is just the chemicals in my brain and I am a good and loving person." EFT will not cure OCD, but it will relieve the psychological issues of self-hatred and depression that result and enable the person to take positive action more easily. If you think you have OCD you should consult a doctor for a diagnosis and to find out what drugs might be helpful to balance your brain chemistry.

Amelia, a successful single woman, lived alone in a four-bedroom condominium. Every room and storage space was packed. After she dealt with her resistance to simplify her clutter, she hired a professional organizer to clear out her home and put her on the right track. It took eight hours to empty just one room! Others find clutter buddies and regularly phone or help each other. Keep reminding yourself that you are not the only one in the world with this problem. If you think your clutter is the expression of emotional chaos find a support group or seek counseling.

Maxine decided to clean out her house incorporating a number of different solutions. First, she joined a clutter support group and found that it was helpful to see that others had the same problem and were available to cheer her on. She picked up some excellent hints for moving forward. She contacted a local charity and made arrangements for them to provide her with a large bin. She set herself a deadline that she would fill the bin within a definite time period. As she filled each bin, it was replaced by a new one. This gave her a sense of satisfaction since she was not throwing things away but passing them on to others in need that would appreciate and make good use of the household items and clothing. As one room after another was put in order and her dining room table finally cleared of all the papers that had covered it for years, she felt confident enough to invite some friends over for dinner.

Photos are challenging for clutterers because they pile up so easily. Many of us don't take the time to organize them. We are fortunate today that with new technology we can put photographs on disks and store them easily. Here too, sorting through pictures and keeping those that best represent an event will help you select a few. This approach is also helpful for people who hoard magazines and newspapers. Pat, a hoarder, paid thousands of dollars to ship boxes of magazines and newspapers including years of unread copies of the Sunday New York Times Magazine sections across the country when she moved from the east coast to California because she was unable to throw them out.

If you keep putting off de-cluttering your life because you feel overwhelmed, the first step is to find out if your clutter could be related to Obsessive Compulsive Disorder or Attention Deficit Disorder. If it turns out to be a chemical imbalance in your brain, help is available through medication or by joining with others who have the same problem. There are groups and websites where information is available.
Start with *www.clutterless.org*

Be kind to yourself. Keep reminding yourself that you are doing the best you can. Emphasize all your positive qualities, and affirm that you can minimize this problem by taking action. You deserve to love yourself and enjoy a happy life.

Appendix II

The Thrill of It All

There is another kind of procrastination that may also be linked to a genetic problem. It involves the compulsion to leave things until the last minute. I'll never forget Serena who wanted me to help her overcome her stress. Serena was an energetic woman who had many interests. She complained that she had so many things to do and so many appointments and meetings to attend due to her community involvements, hobbies and job, that she was always behind and felt frantic.

It was common for her to leave work and try to race across the city during rush hour to get to a board meeting or class. She felt pulled and pressured all the time. There were constant deadlines hanging over her. In our meetings, I tried to help Serena learn to organize her time better. We worked on having her be more realistic about what was achievable. She began to set priorities and let go of some of her commitments. She seemed to be making progress.

Then one day she came in for her session and told me that she was less stressed, but she was not happy. She missed the zing she felt when she made it to a meeting at the last second or tried to beat traffic on her way to a class. The thrill of the challenge was gone, and she wanted it back. She decided to stop trying to change, said goodbye, and left.

I have thought about Serena over the years and wondered about her decision. Then I read an article about thrill seekers explaining that these behaviors may be related more to our biology than psychology. Apparently, some people need more stimulation than most of us in order to feel good. The author labeled them T-type personalities.

Scientists who have studied this problem believe that cortisol, the hormone related to stress, may be a factor. Studies show that low cortisol levels are associated with sensation seeking in men. What stresses other people doesn't stress them. These men tend to "up the ante" to feel excitement. It is possible that thrill seekers are born that way. In 1996, geneticists discovered a "novelty-seeking" gene that relates to the brain chemical dopamine. Dopamine motivates action and can also drive the motor system. The release of dopamine drives us toward a goal, helps energize us, and keeps us focused.

In people hooked on excitement, empty dopamine receptors make them edgy. Dr. Marvin Zuckerman, who has studied sensation-seeking for 40 years said, "To stimulate the system, you have to do something more. That's why sensation-seekers need riskier and riskier thrills to get the same kick." Some of these people resort to drinking, drugs, sex, gambling and other antisocial behaviors. Maybe that's what Serena meant when she said she missed the rush she got when she was trying to juggle all her obligations. Some people get thrills from sky diving, gambling, travel, or partying. Serena created a different kind of excitement to raise her cortisol level.

My theory is that some people who procrastinate and leave things for the last minute are unconsciously creating situations that force them to stress themselves. They have to exert prodigious amounts of energy to complete the task, arrive at the theater as the curtain goes up or get to the airport just before the plane takes off. If that were I, I would be a screaming mess, but these folks seem to take it in their stride. It makes them feel good. They don't seem frazzled or worried. It is just their dopamine at work.

My husband has many T-type characteristics. He invariably leaves his packing for the last minute when he travels. One November morning he threw his clothes into a suitcase at the last minute for a trip from sunny California to snowy Canada only to discover, as the plane landed, that he had left his warm jacket home. Unperturbed, he found a store and bought a new one. It constantly amazes me to see how he is able to rush out the door with zero time to spare to get to an appointment without a worry.

Do you find yourself caught between the thrill of the last minute rush and the negative consequences that you incur as a result? Consider whether you want to continue acting like this or do something about it. Since T-types have a biological tendency to raise their cortisol levels and their dopamine through risky activities, you can begin by becoming aware of your patterns. If they hurt you more than they help you, perhaps you can look for new and different ways to add thrill to your life that do not affect you or others adversely.

Some alternative activities that can fulfill the need for excitement are enjoying intense rock or rap music, watching horror movies, or engaging in travel to adventurous locales. Sensation seeking can also involve extreme sports such as skydiving, hang gliding, scuba diving, auto racing, rock climbing and whitewater rafting. Stop criticizing yourself for being a last minute person. Like Serena, get used to the idea that you need more "thrill" than most people do.

SIX STEPS TO SUCCESS

If you follow these six steps any time you feel stuck and can't move forward with a goal or project, you will see immediate results.

1. **What is my goal?** Name the task, job, or project you want to finish. Check that it is smart. Is it specific, reasonable, attainable and is this the right time to attempt it?

2. **What excuses am I using to avoid completing it**? Say or write down all the excuses you can think of that you are tempted to use to stop yourself from starting, going on with or completing this endeavor. Remind yourself that excuses don't count. Cross them out.

3. **What is the worst thing that might happen if I complete it?** Quiz yourself and keep pushing to discover what your fear thoughts are. Then use EFT when you get to the heart of it.

4. **What belief is stopping me cold**? Review the five main False Beliefs:
   * Failure is unacceptable,
   * People will dislike me if I don't do it right.
   * Success is dangerous.
   * I'm afraid of what the future holds.
   * I don't want to.
   Use EFT on any or all the beliefs that are sabotaging you.

5. **How young was I when I decided this was the truth, and what was going on**?
   Use the Cosmic ATM procedure or try out self muscle testing/pendulum/ideomotor finger methods to discover the age.
   Use EFT to free yourself from the negative results of that memory.

6. **What have I decided to do?** Take action now.

Suggested Reading

Arenson, Gloria, (1981) How to Stop Playing the Weighting Game, NY: St. Martin's Press

_____, (1985) How to Stop Playing the Weighting Game, Mission Hills, CA: Author

_____ (2008) How to Stop Playing the Weighting Game, eBook, Author

_____ (1989) A Substance Called Food: How to Understand, Control and Recover from Addictive Eating. NY: McGraw Hill

_____ (1991) Born to Spend, NY: McGraw Hill

_____ (2003) Born to Spend (New Edition), Santa Barbara, CA: Brockart Books

_____, (2001) Five Simple Steps to Emotional Healing, NY: Simon & Shuster

Ball, Ron (2006) Freedom At Your Fingertips, Fredericksburg, VA: Inroads Publishing

Burns, David D., (1980) Feeling Good; The New Mood Therapy, NY, Morrow

Craig, Gary and Fowlie, Adrienne (1997) Emotional Freedom Techniques: The Manual, The Sea Ranch, CA: Author

Feinstein, David; Eden, DonnaCraig, Gary (2005) The Promise of Energy Psychology; Revolutionary Tools for Dramatic Personal Change; NY: Jeremy P. Tarcher/Penguin

Gallo, Fred, (2000) Energy Psychology: Explorations at the Interface of Energy Cognition, Behavior and Health, Boca Raton, FL: CRC Press

McCarty, Wendy Ann, (2004) Welcoming Consciousness: Supporting Babies' Wholeness From the Beginning of Life, WB Publishing, eBook

Rudin, Ronald A.,(2003) The Craving Brain Second Edition, NY: Quill

Scaer, Robert C., The Body Bears the Burden: Trauma, Dissociation and Disease. Binghampton, NY: Haworth Medical Press

Siegel, Daniel J., (1999) The Developing Mind: How Relationships and the Brain Interact to Shape Who We Are, NY: The Guildford Press

Van der Kolk, Bessel A. (1994) "The Body Keeps the Score: Memory and the Evolving Psychobiology of Post-traumatic Stress," Harvard Review Psychiatry,

Energy Psychology Internet Resources

ACEP: Association for Comprehensive Energy Psychology
www.energypsych.org

Advanced Integrative Therapy (AIT)
www.Seemorg.com

Daniel Benor, MD
www.WholisticHealingResearch.com

Be Set Free Fast
www.BSFF.org

Donna Eden and David Feinstein
www.innersource.net

Emotional Freedom Techniques (EFT)
www.emofree.com

Healing from the Body Level Up (HBLU)
www.jaswak.com

Gloria Arenson
www.gloriaarenson.com

About the Author

Gloria Arenson is a psychotherapist, teacher and award-winning author. She specializes in to helping people overcome compulsive behaviors like spending, procrastination, eating disorders and many others. Gloria conducts classes and workshops internationally and has a private practice in Santa Barbara, California.

www.GloriaArenson.com

QUICK ORDER FORM

Order NOW for friends and family!

You can use this convenient order form for more copies of this book or other books by Gloria Arenson.

Internet Orders: *www.GloriaArenson.com*

Postal Orders: BrockArt Books, 1429 Las Positas Place, Santa Barbara, California, 93105-4525.

Please send the following books. I understand that I may return any for a full refund for any reason.

❑ Procrastination Nation at USD $16.95

❑ Born To Spend at USD $16.95

❑ Freedom at Your Fingertips at USD $19.95

❑ A Substance Called Food at USD $16.95

❑ How to Stop Playing the Weighting Game at USD $9.95

Please send more FREE information on:

❑ Other Books ❑ Speaking/Seminars ❑ Consulting

Name _____

Address _____

City _____ State ___ ZIP _____

Telephone _____

Email _____

Sales Tax: Please add 7.75% for books shipped to CA addresses.

Shipping by air: U.S.: $5.00 for first book, $2.00 for each additional.

International: $9.00 for first book, $5.00 for each additional (Est.).

Printed in the United States
202850BV00001B/277-528/P

9 780962 194252